ORGANIC WEALTH

ORGANIC WEALTH

Create Your Own Slice of Pie

Donald A. Ax

Organic Wealth

Liberty Word Publishing
LibertyWord.com

Wholesale discounts are available. Please contact the publisher.

Printed in the United States of America

ISBN: 978-1-7346656-3-5

This book is dedicated to all who were financially harmed by the imposed COVID lockdowns and to those who want to ensure such a shutdown can't harm them in the future.

The pursuit of profit or income within a free market is what's required for organic wealth creation. Organic wealth is essential in obtaining economic freedom.

Table of Contents

Introduction

Through the end of 2020, according to analysis by Credit Suisse, global household wealth stood at over $418.3 trillion USD.[1] The wealth management bank also projects by 2025 the global wealth of households will be $583 trillion. That's a 39% expansion of new wealth in just a five year span.

The rise in new global wealth will not happen because it drops from the sky or will it be from volcanic lava flows arising out of the earth. But instead, individuals for the most part will create wealth by providing value in their respective economies.

I wrote Organic Wealth because many people believe wealth is distributed unfairly. Further, they conclude a small group of elites are the ones who are able to access the greatest proportion. The rest of society is then left with the little remaining.

While some injustices do occur that disrupt the free market, wealth altogether isn't carved out from some finite source. On the contrary, wealth is generated by everyday people who exchange their labor or talent for a paycheck. Since wealth isn't from some constant source, anyone at any time can create new wealth and add to the global wealth number.

Many of us have to broaden our view of the famous wealth pie. Pieces are not sliced up and served on pretty saucer plates. The wealth pie continually expands from those who meet demand in a marketplace by providing value in exchange for compensation. This book aims to prove this is true.

Since there are many people who assume wealth is distributed unequally, there are some who use that talking point for political purposes. This allows them to push for higher taxation and wealth redistribution policies. It has even progressed to the degree that socialism is viewed as a viable economic system where, they allege, there's fairness and equal outcomes.

The initial three chapters of Organic Wealth will be how wealth is created and how unlimited its formation is. Readers will also learn how they too can expand the wealth pie. Anyone who doesn't know how they can create something from nothing will soon see open doors of opportunity all around. This should encourage even more organic wealth creation.

Moving on from how wealth is created, the next two chapters are regarding the economic environment most conducive to organic wealth and about personal property rights. We'll learn for someone to demand something, they have to supply something. Next, we'll see that private property rights are a prerequisite to reaping the financial rewards of supplying something to a market. This allows income earners to demand other products or to create wealth.

The next portion of this book examines the government utilizing the tax code to confiscate personal property. Of particular interest is the wealth tax and why I contend it's unconstitutional. Once challenged, any attempt to enact such legislation by Congress will be struck down by the Supreme Court. There is a workaround; however, our government leaders could utilize to accomplish much of the same thing. The solution to this is what I dubbed, the Organic Wealth Amendment.

The last three chapters deal with democratic socialism, the Nordic countries and how socialism turns the wealth pie into a zero sum game. We will discover Scandinavian economies aren't even socialist as some claim but rather, capitalist. You will learn further it's not the Nordic Model that's being advanced, but really it's a push for democratic socialism, which will destroy organic wealth creation and make the land barren.

Once you reach the end of the last chapter, please finish by reading the Afterword. This is about what you can do next and how to connect with me online. Now that you have an idea of where we're heading, let's turn the page on this Introduction and jump into the first chapter, *Wealth is Created.*

- ONE -

Wealth is Created

I love blueberry pie, so I certainly don't want just a thin slice of it. Only a large piece will suffice to experience the delicious fresh blueberry filling. If wealth were a finite pie, as some believe, then most of us would be left wanting never able to enjoy a full slice.

It would mean natural resources were the sole filling and valuable land was its crust. Whoever owned or controlled them would be the ones with all the wealth in our society. Natural resources and land are without a doubt a part of existing wealth, but placing value on just these sources is not a complete accounting of wealth.

Most people understand wealth is more than natural resources, but many still believe there's a giant pie of wealth out there that's divided up. They believe the rich owns a majority of what's accessible and the rest of us share the leftover sliver. If you were to ask them, they would maintain wealth is not distributed equitably.

Thanks to the news media, it may just appear it's impossible to have more wealth without the government intervening to achieve some sort of equity. The catastrophe, news reports claim, is the gap between the rich and poor is wider than it's ever been. They say that this widening gap is because the rich almost entirely benefit in capitalism while the poor get left out. The reason is because of the inequitable distribution of wealth in our nation. The takeaways from these reports are that it's unfair and it's the fault of capitalism.

It's not just the news media either. Many on the political far left also see capitalism and free markets as the reason why wealth is not distributed fairly. They want their piece of the pie so they advocate for socialist policies that would give it to them.

This unfair distribution false narrative lacks the understanding new wealth can be created and wealth creation benefits all of us. The great thing about the free market capitalist system of the United States is wealth does not have to be redistributed as those on the far left insist. Rather, wealth can be created organically by anyone at any time. Indeed, you can have a bigger portion of the pie without taking it from someone else.

Unconsumed Income

It's easy to consume income. Nobody needs to hire a professional consumption planner or to listen to some guru on television who's selling seminars on how to spend money. Since spending money is so easy and mindless, it's the default position for most people. Often, as long as we can afford something, any salary is almost entirely consumed trying to fulfill the desire to have the best possible life. It's completely natural for us to want the nicest housing, transportation, clothing and everything else. Therefore, gratification is what drives our spending.

Most Americans spend nearly their entire salary on living for today and find it difficult to see past their next payday. According to a Career Builder survey, 78% of full-time workers live paycheck to paycheck.[1] This means that three out of four people have very little saved.

Even more astonishing, the survey found approximately 10% of those making six-figure incomes lived paycheck to paycheck. When people aren't saving money making two grand per week, they just need to downsize somewhere or seek financial help from a professional.

Living within our means and creating organic wealth will allow us to have a fulfilled life for our entire lives. It's how this American experiment will become a lasting success for ourselves and our children. To ensure the future financial success of the next generation, it's imperative that we teach every child about the dangers of consumer debt (overspending) and, of course, how they can create organic wealth.

I would argue that not saving money over one's lifetime is the main reason why socialism has become so popular within the Democratic Party. Since many people aren't building wealth, some support confiscating it from others who do. There may be some jealous motives, but the main purpose is to either redistribute as direct payments or to fund the left's popular social policies such as free childcare, college and healthcare.

This is going to change with *Organic Wealth*. If you have income, you have the ability to create new wealth for yourself. By following the principles in this book, you will view your income as potential wealth and will direct it suitably so that your financial future is worry free.

Carving finances from our budgets to build wealth need not be painful or distressing. After we do so, we can then live it up with the rest and enjoy today. Your organic wealth adventure begins with your unconsumed income.

It Takes Money

By not consuming all of our salary, wealth can be created through saving and investing. As wealth grows, other investment opportunities present themselves. Maybe it's in real estate, a business idea, a burst asset bubble, low priced shares of stock or some other opportunity. The old adage is true here; *it takes money to make money*.

From time to time there are financial opportunities that can build our wealth. If we're not financially able to take advantage of them, however, we'll miss out. The housing crisis beginning in 2008 is one example of an asset bubble bursting. Unfortunately, many wage earners lost their jobs and their homes because of the financial meltdown. The housing prices dropped like a rock and, as a result, many homeowners were left with underwater mortgages. With no job and unable to sell, the houses became bank owned and vacant.

Having the funds available to buy some of those houses from the banks was a great opportunity back then. Renting them out and waiting for the market to recover, which it did,[2] built a lot of wealth for the saver.

Another bubble burst during the same financial meltdown. The Dow Jones tumbled to a low of 6,443 on March 6, 2009. If you were in the market, you may have been panicking and looking to sell. But as a wealth builder, it was an opportunity to buy low.

In January 2018, about nine years after the stock market crash, the DJIA went over 26,000. In another two years, the Dow surpassed 29,000 and despite the global COVID-19 pandemic, in 2021 it began rocketing well past 35,000. This was a nice return for the contrarian investor who had the capital available to jump in.

Asset bubbles are just one way to build further wealth from savings. If you want to start a business, for example, you'll need capital to get it off the ground no matter how frugal you are or if you do all the work yourself.

Maybe real estate is appealing to you and you're interested in buying an investment property or one to flip for a quick profit. You'll need money for the rehab costs and for the 20% down payment. If you have cash handy, you can do the deal and prosper further.

You never know where or when an opportunity will present itself. You may learn of a new startup company you believe could be the next Amazon or Tesla. Only those who have money saved can invest. It doesn't matter the opportunity, they abound, it takes money to build wealth. To begin with, it's saving your income. Then later, it's exchanging your saved income for investments.

Wealth Creation with Income

When *wealth creation* is used in this book, it's wealth that's derived by saving income. It's not asset appreciation even though appreciable assets can expand your wealth exponentially.

Earning an income can only be considered potential wealth because all of us have the choice to either spend or save the income we earn. Choosing to save is how organic wealth is created. By definition, wealth exists when assets with monetary value exceed debt. But income, unless it's saved, is not considered wealth because it will be consumed on items that don't hold value.

Unconsumed income in *Organic Wealth* is necessarily the main topic because most new wealth first begins as income. If all you ever do is spend your income, you will never have wealth. Wealth creation in this book, therefore, focuses on unconsumed income from either investments or labor.

We can see how wealth is created through unconsumed income by looking at publicly traded companies. Not only does a company have to create revenue (income), but it needs to be profitable (unconsumed income) to be valued by investors. A company spending all its money on expenditures (consumes all its income) will never bring shareholders any value.

This is because when there's nothing left over after their expenses, there cannot be any shareholder distributions or reinvestments in the company to create more revenue. Some unprofitable companies, like Lyft and Uber, are still valued higher because of possible future profits, but these earnings must eventually materialize or their stock price will plummet.

If a company can increase its earnings per share (unconsumed income), its stock price will go up. A higher stock price reflects a company that's worth more. As a result, investors are rewarded with new wealth because the stock has increased in value, which they could sell for a gain. In summary, wealth was created because of increasing income that wasn't consumed.

Thanks to saving income and not consuming it all, everyone can expand their net worth. The question is does this new wealth creation take wealth away from someone else? The good news is no it doesn't because wealth in capitalism is not a zero sum game.

Not a Zero Sum Game

Instinctively, some may believe wealth is a finite pie or a zero sum game. A zero sum game means if one market participant profits then another must lose the equivalent amount because the total value cannot change.

It may be intuitive to think this way because this is what's all around us in the physical world. For instance, the *law of conservation of matter/energy* states matter and energy cannot be created or destroyed in an isolated system. Like in the universe we live in, matter and energy just change from one form to another.

Transactions for products or services are another example of zero sum. A consumer buying groceries spends $100 and the store receives $100. The transaction is a net zero sum, -100 and +100.

If wealth was from a finite source, then whenever someone gained wealth, it would mean another person lost wealth. But that's not what happens. The stock market is a good example for us to consider revealing wealth is not zero sum.

In this market, there's not an equal winner and loser of wealth. Or is it necessary for there to be both a winner and a loser. There can be someone gaining wealth without there being someone losing. Conversely, there can be a loser of wealth without there being another person who gains wealth.

Stock Market

Let's say a newly listed company issues stock for $10/share and Edward buys one share. After a few days, the stock price goes up to $12/share and he then sells his share to Diane. Edward increases his wealth by $2 while Diane has a share of stock worth $12. Nobody has lost anything. Diane's wealth is exactly the same as it was before her purchase. She just exchanged money for a share of stock of the same value. In fact, Edward just created wealth that didn't exist before.

We can look at the previous example from a longer viewpoint. Suppose this newly listed company goes on to do great things and over the next several years they build a very successful business. The earnings of this company grow rapidly in the future compared to from when they first began.

Instead of selling his share of stock soon after buying it, Edward holds on to it. He eventually sells his share in a few years when it's worth $200/share. He would have then made $190/share ($200 - $10). The person buying it at $200 didn't overpay because that's how much the company is worth per share at the time of the transaction. So nobody has lost any wealth. Edward, on the other hand, has created wealth without taking it from someone else. Wealth, as this example shows us, is not a zero sum game.

Transactions

As described earlier, monetary transactions for goods and services are zero sum; a customer pays $100 and a store receives $100. But how do these transactions affect the wealth of both parties, is it zero sum?

If an entrepreneur opens a grocery store and over time becomes wealthy, did the entrepreneur do so at the expense of all the store's customers? Did the customers all become a little poorer so the entrepreneur could become wealthy? If that were the case, then existing wealth would be zero sum, but the correct answer is the customers did not become poorer so the business owner could become wealthy.

Someone buying groceries for $100 did not lose $100, but gained something of equal value, groceries. They consumed their income, but they did not lose anything because at the time of the transaction, the groceries had the same value as the $100. It is true the store owner profited by selling $100 worth of groceries for more than his costs and his expenses. So, the owner did create potential wealth income, but not by a loss of another person's net worth. In reality, if he saved a portion of his income, he created wealth out of thin air.

What happens when the groceries are gone, wouldn't it mean the person has no value left from the transaction and their net worth has declined? It's true in a monetary sense, but the consumer was able to sustain life for a period and that was worth the $100 spent.

If you still contend a transfer of wealth occurred without regarding the value of goods the customers received, then it's still not a zero sum. The store owner didn't gain $100 of wealth at the customer's loss. Actually, the $100 of revenue received covers the cost for the groceries and all the operating expenses for the store. The net profit for the store owner is far less than what was received from all the money spent by the customers.

But this example just points out transactions for goods and services are not a zero sum game as they affect the wealth of the market participants. The truth is the customers didn't lose anything even though they spent a portion of their income. The reason being, they gained something else of equal value. At the time of the transaction, their net worth was exactly the same as before the transaction because the groceries they purchased had equal value.

The store owner received income by using his mind, labor and resources. If the merchant saved some of his income, his wealth would increase over time. It's not a zero sum game because as a result, the customers didn't lose anything.

These two examples reveal to us that wealth creation isn't a zero sum game and there's not a finite pie that needs to be divvied up. Since new wealth isn't dependent upon the loss of others', then this means that any new wealth can be created out of thin air.

Wealth Out of Thin Air

Out of the grassy ground a new seedling has emerged. This new plant owes its creation to windblown cotton and a process called germination. One day, it will become a towering cottonwood tree where squirrels and birds will take refuge under its shaded cover.

A seed from a mature cottonwood tree traveled a great distance through the air on a cottony cloud to find the moist fertile soil. This perfect location allowed the seed's embryo to expand and burst out of its hard exterior. It then began to grow roots to find water before revealing itself to the rest of the world.

If we didn't know any better, this new tree would appear to have been created out of thin air. The yard's gardener didn't germinate a tree and then plant it in the ground in that exact spot. It just grew there on its own.

New wealth that's never existed before is created out of thin air too. There's no government central planner, like a gardener, taking a top-down approach and deciding what an economy may want or need.

On the contrary, new wealth within a free economy comes from people working hard, creating things of value and taking risks with their resources. All of this effort is for the purpose of building something of value for a marketplace to earn income.

To create wealth out of thin air, it not only necessitates income, but it then requires saving and investing. Removing income doomed for consumption and instead investing it creates new wealth right out of thin air. It's a simple in-house transfer of one's own income away from consumption and into savings.

Organic wealth then can be created by anyone with an income. By saving unconsumed income, new wealth is created previously having never existed. It's a new tree that's emerged just like our young and growing cottonwood. There's no need for wealth distribution by the government and nobody else has to lose anything.

Wealth that's Never Existed

The phrase, *wealth out of thin air* conveys it's new wealth and not a wealth transfer from someone else. This is because the income received, which allows for the wealth creation, was in exchange for providing something of equal value such as work performed or selling a product to willing buyers in a market. Because both sides of these kinds of transactions have the same value, a wealth transfer doesn't occur. It's an equal exchange where neither side has lost anything.

Take, for example, an employer hiring someone for their labor. The employer isn't losing its wealth by paying the employee a salary because the money spent is for something of equal value. The employer receives the employee's production, which the company will use to earn additional revenue. Thanks to the employee's labor, the new revenue earned by the company effectively replaces what was spent for that production. Therefore, the money paid out for the employee's salary wasn't a wealth transfer, but an equal transaction because the company's wealth didn't decline.

The employee too hasn't wasted their time because they received money in return. If the employee saves some of their income, then it's brand-new spanking wealth. It never existed before because it was acquired by providing something of equal value in a marketplace and not from being a wealth transfer. The new wealth came directly as a result of their production. Because their labor had a monetary value, any amount that's saved is brand-new wealth that never existed before. Therefore, a near perfect definition of *wealth* would be as such: the saved monetary value of one's labor.

So then, wealth is created out of thin air by first providing value for a marketplace. In exchange for that value, income is earned. Once the income is saved, it becomes new wealth having never existed before. It's not a snap of the fingers, but requires meeting market demand and then being rewarded with income.

Let's illustrate this further with an apple tree that belongs to Owen. The apples have no value until Owen or someone else spends the time picking the apples to sell at a farmers' market.

When Owen sells them, he has created income, which if saved, is wealth that never existed before. It's new wealth because he exchanged something of value, his labor picking apples, which were then sold for income. It was an equal transaction. The people who bought the apples didn't lose anything because they received something of equal value, the apples.

Now suppose Owen hires someone else to pick the apples for him. He pays them $20 per bushel. The person picking the apples is creating new income in exchange for their labor. Owen is losing $20 by paying the person, but now has a bushel of apples of equal value. At this point, the worker has $20 in new income and Owen is even.

Owen can then take his bushel to the farmers' market and sell it for $30. As a result, Owen creates $10 in new income. Of course, the people who bought the apples received something of equal value. They received the ability to eat an apple a day to keep the doctor away. That was worth the $30 in total spent.

The apples' example shows us new wealth can be created having never existed before. The person picking the apples created $20 of potential wealth and Owen created $10 of potential wealth. If each saves their income, the wealth pie would expand by $30. The people buying the apples didn't decrease their net worth because at the time of the transaction, the apples they purchased had equal value to the money spent.

The same way wealth can be created by saving, wealth can also decline. When people sell assets to raise money to consume, the wealth pie shrinks. Most of the time, this occurs when people retire and cash out their retirement accounts such as a 401(k) or an IRA.

Like the windblown cotton, some may not even know it's happening. But every day, people are creating unconsumed income and over time becoming wealthy. Wealth out of thin air isn't something miraculous. It's simply increasing your income and/or reducing your consumption so you have something left over to save and invest. If you change your finances around, you will create wealth out of thin air and make the wealth pie bigger.

The pie gets bigger because organic wealth isn't zero sum. Wealth is created in free market capitalism by providing something of value in exchange for income, which once again, is an equal transaction. Next, taking this money out of the consumption pile and putting it in the asset pile. This income can come from business profits, investment gains, labor or some other way. Creating income, then saving instead of spending, is organic wealth creation.

Meeting Market Demand

I can remember waking up early on weekend mornings and coming downstairs to find my dad watching Bob Ross teach public television viewers how to paint. My dad loved watching him describe his shortcuts on how to paint trees and waves in the water. I too was amazed at his quick art and enjoyed his nice disposition as he taught how to paint landscapes.

The artist wasn't a perfectionist by any means. When he made a mistake, he used to say, "We don't make mistakes just happy little accidents." He would turn his snafu into something fitting wonderfully in his oil painting and his lesson would continue.

Even though Bob Ross's work doesn't sell for millions, we will use his artwork as an example of wealth creation. If Bob Ross painted a desirable piece of art that he could sell for $1,000, then he would be creating new wealth that never existed before.

The person buying the art did not lose their wealth but received something of equal value, the painting. If Bob Ross didn't consume the $1,000, he actually doubled existing wealth. For every painting the late Bob Ross sold for $1,000 and didn't spend, he doubled existing wealth because the $1,000 payments and the paintings had the same value at the time of the transactions.

The paintings aren't consumed like with our previous examples of groceries and picked apples, but hold their value and may even increase in value over time, which would increase the buyer's wealth as well. Selling the paintings for cash wasn't a transfer of wealth from a finite pie. The pie actually grew larger because the artist gained wealth and the buyers didn't lose anything. Each sold painting was an equal transaction.

The only reason Bob Ross was able to sell his paintings was because he met market demand. He couldn't force people to buy his landscapes. The demand for his work must have already existed or there wouldn't have been any paintings sold.

Value in a Marketplace

In order to create wealth in a free market economy, value must be provided to a marketplace which satisfies demand. Bob Ross was able to meet market demand with his oil paintings. In the same manner, all of us can provide value to meet market demand in other ways. We don't need to be a famous artist or even a business owner to create wealth. We just need to bring something of value to a marketplace in exchange for income.

Bob Ross's works are perceived to have value because he was well known, but what about the work of say a machinist? This is someone who gets a weekly paycheck and isn't famous at all. He's a part of a larger manufacturing system that eventually creates a product for his employer to sell. His work is a small part of the finished product, but his work provides value too.

In return for the machinist's skill, labor and time the employer pays him an income. It's an equal transaction. The wages paid by the employer was worth the production value the employer received in return from the machinist. Therefore, the exchange wasn't a wealth transfer. As a result of this transaction, however, the wealth of both parties has the potential to increase.

First, the company selling the finished product creates earnings. If there's profit left over after expenses, the company would have created potential wealth income for its owners. This profit was only possible by previously exchanging a share of the company's capital to pay the machinist for his work. What began as an equal transaction turned out in the end to create wealth for the owners of the company.

Second, the machinist who exchanged his labor and time for a paycheck can also create new wealth. He simply must save part of his income. This unconsumed income is new wealth creation that could only occur by first bringing something of value to a marketplace which satisfied another's demand.

The machinist brought his skill, time and work ethic to an employment market in exchange for income. Anyone in a free market can do the same thing. They simply have to provide value for someone else in exchange for income; this is essential for organic wealth creation.

People in a free economy bring education, training, experience, work ethic and other skills to a labor market to obtain the most income possible. Those who provide more value meeting demand, earn more. For example, college graduates with degrees in high-demand technology fields make more money on average than those with history and art majors.

Similarly, entrepreneurs and investors bring their vision, creativity, hard work and other resources into our capitalist economy. If they provide value that meets market demand, they'll gain profit.

We previously defined wealth as the saved monetary value from one's labor, but this doesn't define other ways that wealth is created. As you may have recognized, the creation of wealth can also occur from businesses and investors who meet demand in return for income or a gain. It's not just from labor income. Thus, a more perfect definition of *wealth* would be: the saved monetary value from meeting demand.

It's easy to see businesses are able to create wealth because they bring products to market that meet demand. The buyers exchange money for a product of equal value they desire. So any saved portion of a company's profits is new wealth for the owners of the business.

This definition of wealth can apply to investments as well. Consider an investor who owns shares of stock that has gone up in value due to a growing company or, rather, one that's meeting demand. A higher stock price is from higher earnings per share (unconsumed income). The increase in shareholder value, therefore, also represents the saved monetary value from meeting demand.

A more straightforward way of looking at stock investments (or any other investment) is if a shareholder sells their stock to another party, then they are meeting demand in the market. Any gain that's not consumed is also the saved monetary value from meeting demand.

To ensure everyone understands where *new* wealth comes from, it's important that we note this definition of wealth. It comes from meeting demand to earn income and then saving a portion of that income. This wealth doesn't come from a transfer or from some sliced up pie.

New wealth for wage earners, business owners and investors then is created organically; all from the bottom-up. The decision whether there's value in a market is ultimately determined by the employer/buyer. In order to create income, it's up to the supply side to satisfy the demand side. Otherwise, there'll be no transaction.

Emphasis on Satisfying Demand

In a free market economy, wealth is created naturally by individuals and businesses. It's not the government saying do this or do that. In order to exchange value for income requires learning what a market may want or need and then providing it. This type of approach in a free economy, where there's an incentive to earn the most income possible, places the emphasis on satisfying demand. The demand must already exist or it must materialize once the supply becomes known and available.

If a market participant wants to earn income, they must satisfy demand or there'll be no transaction. This forces a would-be income earner to adapt, compete, innovate and invent. Capitalism rewards those who meet demand.

Free market capitalism has this emphasis on satisfying demand and it benefits all of us in multiple ways. Market participants on the supply side must compete with one another to meet demand. This competition is what produces lower product prices, better value, desirable features and new products consumers want. As a result, the standard of living for everyone improves.

The workforce likewise has to satisfy demand. Workers compete with other workers to meet the needs of an employer. If they don't meet demand, they could become unemployed and lose their income.

This competition doesn't create slaves, but results in quality employees who help the business be as efficient and productive as possible. Such employees who meet demand in the employment market then help their employers compete against other companies to satisfy marketplace demand to earn revenue for the company.

If there weren't this emphasis, then the marketplace would be inefficient and demand would go unmet. The supply would not be working to fulfill demand because the incentive to try wouldn't be present. There would be less adaption, competition, innovation and invention.

Socialism is an economic system where supply doesn't work to satisfy demand. Supply doesn't try to satisfy demand because socialism removes the incentive for people to be successful by prohibiting earning or accumulating too much. Socialism also guarantees a job or an income, which means removing the incentive for people to provide something of value that others may want or need.

Placing limits on income creation in socialism takes away the incentive to meet market demand because there's no reward for doing so. Additionally, guaranteeing an income takes away the need to adapt, compete, innovate, and invent to create the most income possible. The end result is unmet market demand and a lower standard of living for all of society than there otherwise would be by having the incentive to create income.

Digital Kitties

With socialism, you would never have digital kitties or the next generation of digital assets known as NFTs

(Non-Fungible Tokens). These are unique digital assets distinguishable from other tokens that reside on the blockchain. With this technology you can have tokenized real world assets that provide certificates of authenticity, ownership verification, provenance and other attributes including lien information. In addition, NFTs allow the creation of new digital collectibles such as art, playing cards and even kittens.

In late 2017, a new game was launched, which was the world's first widely used NFT, called Crypto Kitties. These digital cats (not real felines here) breed with other e-cats. The rarer a kitty is the more valuable these digital nothings become. About a month after its launch, with values skyrocketing, digital kitty #1 sold on Dec. 2, 2017 for 246.9 Ethereum (ETH), which is a cryptocurrency worth on that day $114,481 USD.[3] Through the end of 2021, the reported total sales were over 67,000 ETH or the equivalent of about $258 million USD. That's quite a marketplace for just digital kittens.

These NFTs are speculative assets which investors believe will increase in value over time. I would never encourage anyone to blindly buy them without first doing some research. If you believe a project has merit and values will increase, then it may be a good investment.

The company behind these reproducing cats saw a need and filled it. Was the need digital rarity in collectibles, a fun game, a way to invest in digital assets or something else? I don't know, but they met market demand, which created potential wealth income for the company.

The company is creating wealth, but what about the people investing in these kitties, are they building wealth? As long as these things remain collectible and people are willing to purchase them, then it's new wealth creation. It's new because there's demand in the digital kitty marketplace for rarity. Would you rather have $250,000 U.S. dollars or Kitty #1? Some people would say Kitty #1 and that is why it's new wealth. Kitty #1 didn't exist before November 2017.

The NFT marketplace has really taken off; it's now valued in the hundreds of $billions. People see opportunity in them as investments because many have characteristics making them rare and collectible.

Organic wealth is created by earning income as a result of meeting market demand and then saving it, which allows further investment. The income propagation in capitalism expands the wealth pie. There's no wealth transfer like there would be if wealth were a zero sum game because income is earned by entering into equal transactions with willing parties.

- TWO -

Equal Transactions

Free market capitalism balances supply and demand efficiently because it's based on equal transactions. The marketplace produces goods and services in an attempt to provide value to consumers. If something does not, then it will not sell and there'll be no further production. If demand is high, then more supply will be made available to meet the demand. This adaptability to respond to consumer wants and needs is only possible because equal transactions are the only way to earn income.

It doesn't matter what the initial price is, the demand at that price is measurable. The efficiency of the laws of supply and demand makes equal transactions a natural outcome. Both sides of a transaction are equal because the perceived value to a buyer is worth the selling price, otherwise, the transaction wouldn't occur. This is one reason why capitalism is a superior economic system to any other. Over time, the market price accurately balances supply and demand and as a result, each transaction is equal.

The same is true for the employment market. This market doesn't unnecessarily waste capital or waste talent. Someone entering an employment market can earn income once they satisfy the needs of an employer. In return for meeting market demand, both sides agree on an income. It's an equal transaction where both sides have the potential to create new wealth. If a worker's value increases, they can receive a raise or find another employer that will pay them more.

A worker who negotiates for their compensation is the free market at work to achieve market value. Equally true are athletes hiring sports agents to negotiate on their behalf. Similarly, labor unions are not necessarily anti-capitalist either.

If unions exist to negotiate on behalf of workers, that's the free market at work. In my opinion, there are two problems with today's unions, though. First, when market forces change what each employee provides in value, but the terms of the contract doesn't change, then it's no longer an equal transaction. Second, having the power to strike is an unfair tool to gain an advantage that's not market based. A better labor union would be one amenable to market realities and where unresolvable disputes are handled by a neutral mediator.

Equal transactions are how new wealth is created. Organic wealth is nothing but saved income. In order to earn income, equal value must be provided to a marketplace meeting demand. It's the very act of production exchanged for income that expands the wealth pie. In free market capitalism, wealth is indirectly from production and not distributed from a finite source.

You Can Earn an Income

It was a great day for Pontiac G6 lovers when Oprah Winfrey gave her entire studio audience a free one back in 2004.[1] The crowd was sure ecstatic by the surprise gift, jumping up and down with grateful tears of joy while the O shouted at them over and over, "you get a car! And you get a car!" The atmosphere wasn't even electric, it was pure gas powered!

Even if the rest of us didn't receive a car from Oprah, we can do even better. To everyone hoping for a government freebie, winning the lottery or believes the American dream isn't reachable, hear my shout, "You can earn an income! And you can earn an income!" There's nothing stopping most of us. And then, of course, begin saving a portion of our income to create organic wealth.

I'd like to shout this to everyone because income isn't limited by some finite source. Even though there are successful people who are earning large incomes, they're not preventing others from earning an income. Anyone who wants to earn income just has to meet demand.

The idea the American dream is dead and therefore people need socialism is the working of progressive propaganda. The left vilifies the successful regularly by demanding the wealthy "pay their fair share." If you're a socialist, then anything above a deemed acceptable wage would be prohibited. Is this where Progressives want to take us? It sure seems so.

According to the Tax Foundation, in 2018 the top twenty percent of all taxpayers paid 68.9% of all federal taxes. The bottom forty percent had a negative effective federal tax rate; they received more than what they paid.[2] As for the richest income earners, the top one percent paid 25.9% of all federal taxes. I would argue if the richest 20% contributed the same as the bottom 80%, then that would certainly be a fair share. But in reality, they're paying more than twice as much (68.9% to 31.1%).

This is not a critique of the progressive tax system, but pushing back against socialist ideas. The left's battle cry isn't really about raising government revenue from untapped sources but rather, to progress toward some notion of equity. Their policies, though, never aim to expand the numbers of people who would become successful and self-reliant. It seems their goal is to bring people down who, according to them, earned too much; it's also to create government dependents out of the rest.

Policy agendas limiting income and organic wealth creation come right out of socialism. According to Alexandria Ocasio-Cortez (D-NY), a system (free market capitalism) allowing people to become billionaires is immoral.[3] Her fix is a 70% marginal tax bracket for the highest earners. Elizabeth Warren (D-MA) and Bernie Sanders (I-VT) believe excessive wealth accumulation is unjust and should be reined in by taxing wealth. If their policies are implemented, over time, the confiscation would certainly go deeper and wider and affect many more people. There's much more about the wealth tax in the chapters ahead.

These socialist ideas seem to conclude having too much wealth is simply wrong and not that they truly believe we need a fairer tax system. If progressives get their way, then no one would ever be able to accumulate what the government rulers surmise is too much wealth because the tax system would prevent it.

What progressives don't understand is people who earn high incomes do not take away the opportunity for others to earn an income. The reason is simply because income is earned in equal transactions; it's not divvied up.

A Worthy Activity

In a free economy, when someone within a marketplace has a need, income can be created by another party who can fulfill that need. This makes creating income a worthy activity because those earners are in effect solving other people's problems.

Bill Gates is someone who met market demand. He was at one time the richest person in the world as the co-founder of Microsoft. Others have since overtaken him, but he's still very wealthy. Does Bill Gates deserve to be a multi-billionaire? He met market demand for computer software and cloud services so the answer is yes.

The customers who exchanged their money for the Windows operating system didn't lose anything, but gained something of equal value improving their business or standard of living. The billions Bill Gates has earned were for providing equal value to millions of people. All these transactions were equal.

In early 2019, Mr. Gates said, "I don't deserve my fortune, nobody does. It has come through timing, luck, and through people I worked with. I certainly worked hard and I think software has been a beneficial thing, but I benefited from a structure too."[4]

His political correct answer is more about appeasing a woke crowd who're looking to burn rich witches rather than a worthy critique of capitalism. The structure Gates benefited from was a free market. If the government put the brakes on the ability to generate income, then the next Microsoft won't even come into existence, and customer demand will go unmet. Having unmet market demand doesn't help society, but prohibits true progress.

Because the free market structure existed, the computer generation began and changed our world for the better. Furthermore, many would argue the Bill & Melinda Gates Foundation has the opportunity to accomplish more with their fortune than bureaucrats in Washington D.C.

Free market capitalism is morally superior to other economic systems because it's based on equal transactions. Nobody loses anything because both sides are equal. Earning income isn't a nefarious activity because it's done by meeting market demand. If there weren't people willing to buy what was being offered, the transactions wouldn't take place.

High income earners, therefore, shouldn't be targeted by politicians as some sort of evil doers who need their income generation activity curtailed. Their only crime is meeting the demand of a marketplace which is a good thing not a bad thing. One can only earn income in a free market by exchanging something else of equal value another party desires.

Socialism, yes the democratic kind too, is not made up of equal transactions. Income is distributed, not earned in a free market. This distribution of income comes from a source declining over time. Thus, a wealth pie that shrinks and an ever decreasing standard of living for everyone, except of course, the government elites. You can read more about unequal transactions in the last chapter, *Zero Sum Wealth.*

The left seem to have the socialist model in mind when they claim income inequality. It's as if they believe income needs dividing up and the benefits of our free market aren't obvious to fair observers. These leftists should stop thinking and talking like socialists.

High income wage earners are paid what the free market is willing to pay them. If someone provides value that meets market demand, then they should be rewarded with however much the market will bear. The beautiful attribute of free market capitalism is the income earned by one person doesn't prevent someone else from earning income too. It's all about meeting demand; not slicing up a finite pie.

Earning income by meeting demand is an equitable action. Nobody loses and both sides win. It's how organic wealth is created in a free economy, and is something needing encouragement not vilification. These equal transactions, not only create organic wealth, but incentivize everyone to earn income.

Incentivized to Earn

The opportunity in capitalism to create income is what drives our economy. When people believe they can be successful earning money, their animal spirit awakens. The urge to meet demand in a marketplace becomes their primary goal. As such, successfully earning income satisfies this hunger and fulfills their need to be productive and self-reliant.

John Maynard Keynes, the British economist whose theories Keynesian economics are based upon, used the term, animal spirits, to describe human emotions in connection to a volatile market. Nowadays, animal spirits is also used to convey the human response when there are favorable circumstances to create income. In other words, it means if you see it, get up and go get it.

Because of our created nature, humanity capitalizes on possibilities. It's why roads, bridges and ports are built. It's why the Old World dispatched ships to explore the earth in the hopes of finding new trade routes and sources of natural resources like spices and gold. Today, it's why scientists are employed to discover how we may conquer new frontiers such as Mars and traveling asteroids to mine their raw materials.

When the opportunity exists to improve commerce or one's earning potential, then naturally we as a people get up and go. This natural desire to improve is why free market capitalism works. The free market gives people the liberty to see opportunity and then meet demand; not for the sake of meeting demand, but for the sake of their own financial benefit. If the price is right, a capitalist will fill the need; a kill two birds kind of thing or rather, an equal transaction where both sides win.

Socialism, in contrast, places roadblocks to the paths leading to financial success countering our human nature. It seeks to make society become government dependent rather than self so. But as resources dwindle and the promised wealth equality fantasy fades away, hopelessness and poverty spread like a plague.

Free market capitalism works with our human nature not against it. As a result, a free people with the incentive to create income will foster an unlimited number of equal transactions. These transactions are win-win and make the wealth pie grow.

Competition for income in free market capitalism is what gives all of us the opportunity to create income. We just have to meet market demand whether working as an entrepreneur or working as an employee for a company that's competing with other businesses.

The profit motive in a free market encourages competition. No single company has a lock on attempting to satisfy demand. Other companies will compete for any market share that may exist all with the desire to earn income. These actions of meeting demand are good for all of us because innovations and new products are introduced improving our lives.

Workers have this same incentive to earn income; which is why they are educated, trained and become the best employees as possible. They do so to meet their employer's needs in order to earn as much income as possible.

After meeting demand, workers then can move up the ladder to another job, which leaves a position open for someone else. Upward mobility is an important characteristic of capitalism. It allows equal opportunities for workers and higher wages for those who continue to meet employer demand.

If businesses are meeting market demand and more workers will help generate greater revenue for their business, then they will hire additional people. Companies that are incentivized to earn income by satisfying customer needs will create a vibrant job market. A competitive job market results in higher wages, increased employment opportunities and upward mobility for all economic classes. This incentive to earn income fits perfectly within free market capitalism.

Capitalism is by far the fairest economic system in existence because it's based on equal transactions where demand is met because people are incentivized to earn income. Workers are not stolen from or enslaved. They provide skills, work and time in exchange for a paycheck which is determined by the free market. In like manner, businesses can only sell products and services once they meet demand.

Organic wealth is created from equal transactions where both sides benefit. These equal exchanges never reach a point of exhaustion between supply and demand because demand will never be fully satisfied. Thus, the supply side is continually trying to entice the demand side. As a consequence, they introduce new and innovative products and services leading to a better quality of life for everyone.

Better Quality of Life

Earning income is just one side of an equal transaction. The other side is the buyer. A free market based on equal transactions makes life better and more enjoyable for everyone including the side consuming their income. This is because the products and services offered by businesses satisfy society's needs and wants.

In capitalistic economies, businesses exist to make a profit. Because of this, there's a built in incentive to create products and services customers will want to purchase. This is the only way a business can earn income; otherwise, a company will cease to exist.

The end results are businesses which continually work to satisfy consumer demand. This requires understanding what a market may want or what it would need. If a company isn't concerned about meeting ever changing demand, another one will successfully step in and take their market share.

The competition between companies to meet demand benefits all of us. The companies which can satisfy market needs and wants, gain revenue, but the real winners are the consumers. We get better products, services and experiences, which improve our lives.

The consumer has the power. It's because the consumer has the choice to either enter a transaction or not, is why businesses compete with one another with offerings attempting to meet demand. As a result, the standard of living for society as a whole continually gets better.

A great example of this is the long time brick and mortar retailer, Kmart. It wasn't just Amazon that cleaned their clocks; there were other retailers too. Kmart began losing market share first to Target and Walmart. These two retailers were able to meet market demand, which Kmart couldn't identify or if they did, they just couldn't change their brand's perception to the public.

Shoppers who want "Always Low Prices" will choose Walmart. While shoppers who are price conscious, but also want on-trend product offerings are attracted to Target's brand promise, "Expect More. Pay Less." Of course, Amazon satisfies those who want convenience.

Kmart was king for a time, but as other companies found ways to compete, it began its decline. A bad outcome for the *blue light special* store, but beneficial to the consumer. Our shopping experiences have improved with options like Walmart, Target and Amazon. Would we want to settle with a single option that wouldn't reinvent itself by meeting shopper demand?

Which retailers will prevail in the post-COVID future? It will be the brands attracting customers by offering products, prices and shopping experiences the customer desires. They then must consistently deliver on that value. In capitalism, the consumer ultimately wins because it's incumbent upon the supply to satisfy the demand.

If you ask successful entrepreneurs how to come up with a business idea, no doubt their answer would include, "solve a problem" or "fill a need." Many people answer that question by saying, "do what you love," but in order to have success, you have to meet demand regardless if you love it or not.

The Poor are Not Left Behind

How about those in poverty? With wealth creation by others, do the poor get poorer or are they harmed in any way? With organic wealth creation, the poor, as a result, do not get poorer as some on the left seem to imply.

On the contrary, entrepreneurs with a profit incentive create things of value and make our economy grow. A growing economy creates job opportunities and possible upward mobility for all economic classes, which includes those currently in poverty. A tight labor market will lift people out of poverty more than any government handout ever could. Not only upward mobility, but the standard of living for the poor actually improves with free market capitalism.

Free market capitalism improves the lives of those who are considered poor and has lifted much of the world out of extreme poverty. Would you rather be poor in 1900 or poor today? Most of those currently in poverty have enough food and, like the rest of America, usually eat too much not too little. They live in uncrowded housing, utilize smartphones, enjoy streaming services and own cars transporting them to a job or through a drive-thru fast-food restaurant. That's far better than the poor's plight back in 1900.

There are still, of course, problems of homelessness and other crises. These cases, though, are not the majority of those in poverty but only a minority. Additionally, if people who are in such crises want and seek help, issues like homelessness and food shortages are usually temporary. Even though some fall through the cracks, they don't have to stay there. Organic wealth creation in free market capitalism has been, and still is, the answer to poverty in our world.

Our economy has produced goods and services improving the lives of all citizens not just those who are rich. It's because of the profit motive from free market capitalism that entrepreneurs have the ability to create things that even those with the lowest of incomes can take advantage of to obtain a better quality of life.

Wealth Accumulation

As the introduction of this chapter mentions, expanding the wealth pie with equal transactions is a characteristic of capitalism. Providing value to a market will earn income, which if saved, is new wealth creation. Accumulating wealth, therefore, is the benefit and right of all citizens of a free economy and shouldn't be forsaken by anyone no matter their income level.

A point of concern lately from academia and news media outlets is the number of new millionaire households the U.S. economy is churning out. There were a record 13.6 million households in 2020 with a net worth of at least one million dollars. That's an increase of 7.4% from the previous year in 2019.[5] The number of new millionaire households has increased each year for the past ten years. The number of those who are considered affluent grew to 32.3 million in 2020. These are households with a net worth of between $100,000 and $1,000,000, not including personal residences. As of 2020, there are a total of 128.5 million American households and 35.7% of them are affluent or worth more than $1 million.

With the most millionaire households ever comes the comparison of how little wealth the working and middle classes have accumulated. "Wealth inequality is rising in America," they warn us and "It's not right so much wealth is in the hands of so few."

They say this as if the wealthy grabbed all the gold before anyone else with a pick and shovel had a chance to start digging. The truth is, with organic wealth creation, anyone at any time can mine for gold.

It's important for everyone to accumulate wealth no matter their income level. Building wealth will provide financial security and a better standard of living. This is especially true once retirement age is reached.

Generally, cash is not a good long term investment because money's purchasing power decreases over time because of inflation. There are good reasons, however, to be in cash like with your emergency fund, saving for other investments or saving for a future purchase, e.g., a family vacation.

Wealth accumulation therefore is buying or exchanging money for other assets. These other assets provide benefits depreciating cash in your checking account cannot. Depending on what you accumulate, they may appreciate in value and/or provide income.

It's just common sense those with more disposable income could invest more and accumulate more wealth. We should be thankful there are so many investment opportunities in our economy. This increase in millionaires is an outcome that's good not bad.

It was difficult for the working and middle classes to invest when wages were stagnant over the previous decade before Trump's economy. At the same time, prices were rising especially for health care. It's no wonder budgets were squeezed. And if people didn't downsize, there was nothing left over. As a result, many couldn't invest much to build wealth.

The fact there's some people who have been creating wealth all along isn't the problem. The real issue is moderate income earners can't save enough to invest. This has nothing to do with those who can save some unconsumed income.

Wage growth in our economy is the answer which occurs when there's competition for employees in a tight labor market. Wage growth and unconsumed income will allow more wealth accumulation for all economic classes.

Instead of lamenting there are nearly 10% of American households that are worth over $1 million, we should be celebrating this fact, and questioning how can we double or triple those numbers. These days, many in our society want government to do many things, but what's needed is for our public leaders to encourage organic wealth creation from the time people enter the workforce. This objective should be highly prioritized to prevent future dependents and to lower costs to the taxpayer.

If large numbers of households were building wealth, then we wouldn't need to worry so much about an empty social security trust fund or how people will pay for health care. Wouldn't it better if people could take care of themselves? Those then who don't have the resources could use society's safety net.

Many of the new millionaire households in 2017 through 2021 were most likely assisted by the rising stock market and higher real estate values. For instance, the Dow Jones increased by 56.7% from 22,744 in Jan. 2017 to 35,650 in Dec. 2021.

The substantial increase in stock portfolios propelled a lot of retirement accounts and made many new millionaires. Helping too was housing prices have reached all-time highs in many areas of the country. More people creating wealth is what we should want and something we should encourage not discourage.

Begin Wealth Accumulation Today

In order to double or triple the number of wealthy individuals, many more income earners need to begin saving and investing. That's clear. One of the goals of this book is to inspire people to create new wealth they otherwise wouldn't have. That's why the remainder of this chapter is all about your personal organic wealth creation. Then one day, the future success stories written on how there are many new millionaires in our economy will include you, an Organic Wealth reader. If you want to skip ahead, we'll get back to the macro level in chapter three.

To get to the financial destination you dream of, it's going to take *front-loading*. This means doing much more right now so you can reap the financial benefits later in life. Working 40 hours per week and consuming almost all the take home income will not be enough to make any dreams come true.

Instead, front-loading will require sacrifice, hard work and risk taking. By doing these things, it will result in a future payoff making the work and sacrifice worth it. Don't put this off. There's nothing more satisfying than gripping the reins of your life and ordering it in an intentional way. So start today and gain control. It's the beginning of wealth creation.

Front-loading isn't just for twentysomethings either. You can begin right now no matter your age. It's never too late to sow on the front end to reap a harvest on the back end. You may have just been consuming all your income, going with the flow and hoping for the best. But this is a formula which will result in the opposite of front-loading.

Hoping for the best without a plan is ensuring the continuation of the status quo. Without front-loading your life, you're in jeopardy of back-loading it, which is continuing to work well into your retirement years because there's been very little wealth created.

What's the greatest obstacle to creating substantial organic wealth? It's not ability or opportunity; it's the status quo and putting off front-loading until tomorrow. So now that we're ready to front-load, let's look at sacrifice, hard work and risk.

Sacrifice

We all feel good when we sacrifice for other people. When we help a person in need, we're sacrificing our time, our plan and sometimes our money. The return is worth it knowing we've made a difference in someone's life even if it was a small thing.

Sacrificing for your future self can also bring positive feelings of doing the right thing. Just think how selfish your former self was for not considering you today. If only we could go back in time and sarcastically say, "Thanks a lot!" That's not in our power to do. But what is in our power is to make changes now so our future self will truly be thankful.

How do we sacrifice for the future? We can live within our means and create more unconsumed income to save and invest. Also, we can use our time and talents to increase our potential wealth income instead of using all of our free time on other things. There has to be a balance between work and fun, but sacrificing for our future self can be very fulfilling.

Hard Work

It takes hard work to increase income. But working more today will mean less work in the future. And better than that, being able to do what we want with our free time is an essential goal of front-loading. We don't want to just get by in retirement. We want to be in the financial position to do whatever brings us joy such as traveling, hobbies and sharing with others.

Hard work may mean a new business idea, a side hustle, inventing a new product or creating something else of value such as writing a book. To begin with, your work may involve becoming an eBayer. This is someone who sells their unused or unneeded stuff on eBay to raise capital. Monetizing past consumption takes work, but it's very rewarding getting some of your money back.

Risk Taking

Without risk, there is no reward. It's a cliché, but also very true. Let me now offer a generalization: the greater the risk potential, the greater the reward potential. Front-loading your life will mean some risk taking to increase your income. Like me, you may take the time to write a book. This certainly involves risk it won't sell or the book won't be liked. There are also upfront costs in getting it published and marketed so it's not just your time you're risking. Additionally, the time invested for any new undertaking means missing out on other opportunities to create income.

Endeavors like starting a business, investing or buying a rental property will involve risks. The key is not taking too large of risks such as with day trading or jumping in without doing your homework. Educated risks can be very rewarding, but it requires learning and preparation. When you're beginning something new, having a mentor or knowing someone who's done it already can mitigate rookie mistakes and set you up for success. Seek those people out and ask for their support. Doing so will pay off many times over and lead to success sooner.

Compounding

The worst time to begin thinking about retirement is when your coworkers begin wondering how long you're going to stick around. If your answer is you just love to work, it probably means you didn't front-load your life or your investments. Let not that become you.

The best time, of course, is when you first enter the workforce. Investing your savings from when you're young takes full advantage of compounding. The more time you have to save and invest, the more compounding will grow your money.

Compounding is interest earned and then reinvested with the original principle to earn more interest. For example, if you invest $10,000 for twenty years at 8% interest (compounded annually with no additional deposits), your balance will grow to $46,609. If you double the time to forty years, your balance will become $217,245. As you can see, compounding for an additional twenty years grows your investment exponentially.

To get compounding to work for you to create exponential growth not only requires time, but it requires front-loading. It doesn't matter if you're starting later in life. By front-loading your investments, as much as is possible right now, will allow you to receive the most benefit from compounding.

There are several avenues to compound. You can earn interest on your principal when you loan money such as with CDs, U.S. Treasuries, money market accounts and private lending. You can also compound by buying dividend-paying stocks. When companies pay a dividend, you can use those proceeds to purchase more stock.

Investing in the broader stock market on a regular basis is kind of like compounding. Your ongoing investment may not earn interest, but it will, on average, appreciate due to the earnings of the corporations in your portfolio being reinvested to grow their businesses.

Maximizing Earnings

Deciding to front-load will require a new way of thinking. A good place to start is to begin looking at your personal finances as if it's a business. Doing so will align your personal objective so it's the same as of a business owner. Successful businesses attempt to *maximize earnings*, which is the same thing as increasing their net profit. It's not they don't care about anything else, but the main purpose of a business's existence is to profit as much as is possible.

To be most effective, maximizing earnings requires a two-pronged approach. The first method is to reduce expenses to become as lean as possible. The second, of course, is to create more income.

Maximizing your earnings will allow you to become wealthy much sooner and receive the freedom it brings. You won't have all the answers just yet like how you're going to increase your income. But you can start the process at this moment. So let's begin!

The place to start is to determine how much money you have available to save every month. This is just a beginning amount before you maximize your earnings. In order to see this amount, though, you'll need to create a budget—if you don't already have one.

If you have a 401k or other retirement plan from your employer, you may want to contribute as much as possible to their plan especially if your company has a match benefit. A company match can really fuel your retirement plan. Play around with compounding and your employer's match to see its true value over time.

Creating a budget is tedious but a necessary first step. You can write it down on paper, use a word processor or spreadsheet. First, list your monthly take-home income. After that, list all your outlays per month, including a monthly breakdown of periodic expenses like property taxes and gifts. The amount left over is what you currently have to save each month. These are the seeds for future wealth creation. Enter this amount in the *savings* line-item in your budget.

Reduce Expenses

The next step is to look over your expenses and find ways to cut and downsize. Do you really need your cable TV package? Maybe you can get by with a cheaper plan or you can cut the cord altogether. Instead, buy a Roku box to stream Netflix or YouTube TV. Perhaps you can be happy with a digital TV antenna to watch over the air channels. All those channels are totally free.

There are many ways you can cut back to increase your savings every month. Not only cable, but consider cutting back salon visits, clothing purchases, gym memberships, miscellaneous subscriptions, your cellular contract, buying coffee out and eating at restaurants. Look over your budget, what else did your carefree "employee" get you into you can reduce or eliminate?

Reducing your expenses will free up as much money as possible and maximizes your earnings. The goal here is to create a fixed saving plan not fluctuating every month. In other words, execute the plan like the owner of your own business. Remember, front-loading takes sacrifice today for a future payoff... no pain, no gain.

Can you downsize your car, your house or where you pay rent? Really think out of the box. Some mothers would love to have their child eat dinner with them every night. Free room and board is a nice place to begin front-loading (not to be confused with free-loading). Don't worry; you can pay your parents back by having a solid plan to be successful and independent. The point is, determine if radical downsizing is a possibility to loosen up some real cash.

In addition to cutting from your monthly budget, you can really get things moving by selling previous years' consumption. Consider liquidating any big-ticket items too like jet skis, motorcycles, campers and boats. After all, they're depreciating every year so why not raise some capital to create wealth?

You'll be surprised by the amount of money you can make by learning how to sell things on Craigslist and eBay, among other apps that bring buyers and sellers together. There's a gold mine within most households of stuff not necessary to hold on to anymore. With all the money you'll receive from selling all the junk, you'll be well on your way to reaching your next goal.

Increase Income

Once you've created a budget, cut some expenses and are selling things to raise capital, it's time to increase your income. If you're exchanging your time for a paycheck, it makes sense to earn as much as possible for your time.

Check out if there are other positions at your company you could apply for that pay more. It may require getting additional training or certification, but why not do it? You're there for eight hours anyway. Remember to operate like a business and don't be intimidated or unwilling to leave your comfort zone. If there are no better opportunities available, try looking elsewhere. Despite the effects of government shutdowns, economic downturns and progressive socialist policies; the U.S. economy still has employment opportunities available to pursue. At least it did at the time of this writing.

In addition to increasing your employment income, you may be thinking to yourself about how else you can create new income with your free time. I'm flattered, organic wealth is a twinkle in your eye. There are side hustles available for just about anyone. There are too many apps to list here, but consider making extra money with your time by taking advantage of TaskRabbit, Thumbtack, Wag!, Airbnb, Doordash, Postmates, Grubhub, Instacart, Shipt, Turo, Lyft and Uber.

After working so hard, you're now a lean mean financial machine. The savings line-item in your budget should be looking much better and your savings balance must appear fatter thanks to all the sales of the fun and cool things from times past. Are you a millionaire yet? Hardly, but you're not done yet either. With an ongoing savings plan, compounding and new opportunities to earn more income, it's more likely to happen than it otherwise would have been.

- THREE -

Unlimited Wealth

Some may believe there's a limit to the amount of wealth that can be created because of a limited money supply. But that's not the case. Wealth isn't restricted by our fiat currency because the Federal Reserve can always increase the money supply as growth warrants. Even when we were on the gold standard, the money supply could increase with additional gold mining or by revaluing gold higher as the U.S. did in 1934.[1]

In our fiat system, the Central Bank increases the money supply by encouraging borrowing primarily through the discount rate. It can also buy government securities in the open market, which is almost like printing new paper money.[2] Another method the Fed uses is to lower the reserve requirements so banks can lend out more.

Conversely, when an economy is overheating and inflation is rising, the Fed can decrease the money supply. They accomplish this by discouraging lending by raising the discount rate and by selling Treasury debt instruments, which removes money from the system. The Federal Reserve may also sell other assets it has on its balance sheet to remove money from the economy.

The Federal Reserve uses the M2 measurement to determine how much money is in the economy.[3] This includes M1, which is cash and checking deposits, but also includes other assets that are highly liquid, but not quite as liquid as cash such as savings deposits.

In October 1991, the M2 was $3.36 trillion.[4] In October 2021, it was $21.2 trillion. The money stock increased by 530% in 30 years. In the same period, by comparison, the GDP increased by only 270%. Because of the pandemic and the massive stimulus, the M2 money stock has increased even more sharply.

The following chart shows the growth of the money supply over thirty years from 1991 to 2021. The money stock will never prevent new wealth because the Fed can always create more or loose money it has in reserve to facilitate actual growth through lending.

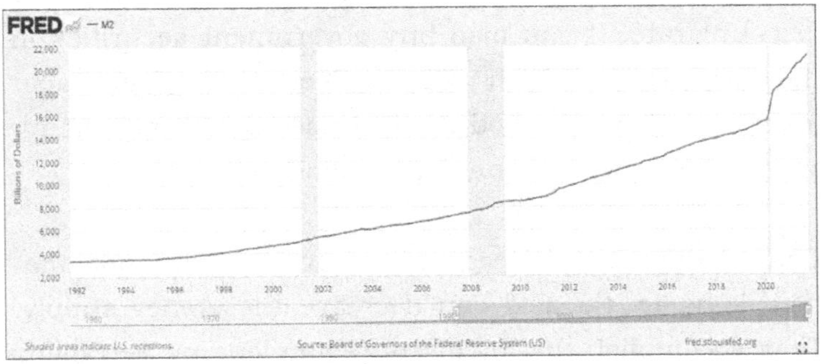

It's important to mention that M2 isn't a measurement of wealth. Our money's primary purpose is to be a medium of exchange to further transactions. The value market participants provide to others is how wealth is created where money earned can be exchanged for assets.

Now that we know the money supply isn't an issue, what about our income potential? With free market capitalism, income creation is unlimited.

Consumption to Income

We've grown accustomed with the word *unlimited.* It's not hyperbole anymore. Our cellular, text and data plans are advertised as unlimited. Although these services are said to be unlimited, it doesn't mean infinite data use is possible though. It just means enough resources are available for normal customer activity. As a mobile company's user base grows, so will the resources available grow to satisfy those needs.

With free market capitalism, unlimited income is possible as well. It doesn't mean each of us can earn one million dollars a year without there being hyperinflation. It just means for as long as a person or company meets market demand, they will earn income. And, the more businesses and people there are who meet market demand, the more income that will be created.

Accordingly, if there are millions of people earning millions of dollars each by meeting demand, it will not prevent anyone else from earning income. They likewise just have to meet demand. There is no limit to the potential of earned income for those meeting the needs of a market.

The key making unlimited income possible is consumption. Whenever someone consumes their income, it becomes income for somebody else. When people spend their money, it circulates throughout the economy as consumption and then income again.

If people aren't spending money in an economy, however, the income generation cycle ends. This was most notable during the COVID-19 lockdowns when millions of people were forced to stay home. A large percentage of the income received just went into checking accounts or it was used to pay down debt instead of going to consumption.

Notwithstanding startup capital or borrowed money, workers earn income when their employers first consume its income. By paying salaries and wages, income is created for employees. As a consequence, as these workers spend their money, it becomes income for others.

Say Ethan works at a job and receives a $500 paycheck. He then spends it all at Best Buy, which means Best Buy received $500 in income. What began as income for Ethan became income for Best Buy besides because Ethan had a job and consumed his paycheck.

Best Buy then consumes the $500 by paying Olivia, its employee, $500 in wages. Olivia goes out and spends her after tax income at the grocery store, gas station and uses the rest to help pay her rent. These three companies then consume their portion, which is income for another person or vendor and so on and so on. All these transactions are *consumption = income.*

The after tax amounts from the $500 gets recycled repeatedly until someone rescues it from consumption and saves it, which is organic wealth creation. As we can see, income is generated each time a person or a business consumes their income. The more of these transactions that occur the more income will be created.

Unless income is saved, this money will be exchanged for other things having equal value like labor, food and rent. In the $500 example above, the money supply wasn't a factor. It was the same money that was received as income and then consumed for other things. This money cycled, also known as the *velocity of money,*[5] through the economy as income and then consumption five different times. The more it does get consumed in equal transactions, the more total income will grow.

The reason consumption takes place is that the marketplace offers products and services people need and want. Members of society desire a better quality of life so products and services that provide value are obtained through consumption of income.

Multiplying Income

Whenever *new* money is introduced into the income/consumption cycle, it multiplies its effect until it's saved once again. As we'll soon see, this new money can come from a variety of sources. One reason new money is introduced is because of a strong economy. A growing labor market introduces new money into the cycle due to new position hiring and wage growth. As a result, people become more confident and spend more. All of this economic activity multiplies throughout our economy.

Let's look at an example. Mia is feeling confident about her future earnings potential because of a good labor market and decides to buy a handcrafted bag on Etsy for $200. She used her credit card to get the 2% cash back. Good grief, Mia!

The Etsy shop gained $200 in new income because Mia was confident in the economy and decided to splurge on an unneeded item instead of only her usual consumption. Now let's say the Etsy shop owner takes the $200 in new income and spends it at macys.com. Macy's then has $200 in income it otherwise wouldn't have had without Mia falling in love with a handbag. At this point, total income has increased by $400 all because Mia consumed more than usual.

That's not the end of the $200 either because let's say Macy's will consume it with a vendor to replenish stock that was sold. The vendor then has $200 in income. So now, what started out as just $200 in new income has grown to $600 with three different entities and it's just getting started.

The above example reveals that an increase in consumption because of confidence, higher wages or new hires, not only increases income but multiplies it. If the money remains in the income/consumption cycle, total income can increase exponentially. This is because consumed income isn't destroyed, but becomes income for someone else. The more of these transactions taking place, the greater total income will be.

Trillion Dollar Companies

In August 2018, Apple became the first U.S. company to be worth a trillion dollars according to their market cap (stock price x outstanding shares).[6] Amazon was the second in the United States to reach the trillion dollar valuation a month later. Microsoft, Alphabet (Google), and Tesla have also since then reached the $trillion threshold with Microsoft surpassing $2-trillion in 2021.

It took Apple only two years to become the world's first $2-trillion dollar company in 2020 after reaching the $1-trillion valuation. As of autumn 2021, Apple is closing in on the $3-trillion mark.

These five companies receive billions of dollars of revenue (income) every year. Even so, there is still room in our economy for even more trillion dollar companies vacuuming up billions of dollars yearly. This potential can't happen all at once, but over time as our economy grows larger.

The reason this is possible is because of consumption. The expenditures of these behemoths account for most of their income. So what doesn't get paid out in salaries and wages (income for employees), gets paid out to suppliers and vendors, which becomes income for those companies. Also we cannot forget the tax revenue generated that's paid to all levels of government. This too is consumed and becomes income again.

The net income (net profit) of the largest four companies gets recycled too. Amazon and Alphabet do not pay dividends to shareholders.[7] Instead, they use their profits for expansion through capital expenditures and acquiring other companies like Amazon buying Whole Foods. These investments, though, become income to other parties.

Apple and Microsoft do pay dividends and they buy back shares of their own stock. Any profits paid out as dividends become income to their shareholders. The buyback plans of both these companies increases the share price for their shareholders and becomes income to those who sell their shares back to Apple and Microsoft.

The end result is most of the billions in revenue find its way back into our economy as income to another party where it could be consumed. The only exception is the cash saved that's never put to use. However, banks use these deposits to loan out to people or other entities so a large portion does make its way back into the economy's income/consumption cycle.

This doesn't take into account international operations. These five global companies receive income from and pay expenses to other markets, which means income and consumption from outside the United States.

The income/consumption cycle allows the potential for an unlimited number of billion or trillion dollar companies in our economy. There will never be a shortage of income available to spend because as consumption occurs, it turns into income again available for further consumption. It's the income/consumption cycle at work. The caveat to this potential is a company must be able to meet market demand. If they are able to meet it, they will earn income.

This income/consumption cycle is why a free market economy has unlimited income potential. For as long as people and businesses continue to consume because of met market demand, income is once again created.

The Income Pool

To illuminate this, picture the income/consumption cycle as a giant pool of water that just keeps churning. The pool is money representing both consumption and income. The money within the pool is both because while it represents income to one party, at the same time it's consumption to another. To the one where it represents income, it soon will be spent and represent consumption. It's important to note the money in this pool isn't wealth but goes back and forth as income and consumption.

The income pool is always swirling about and just changing hands, but the volume isn't static. What flows in is new money consumed from loans and liquidation of assets. This new money adds to the volume of the income pool so even more money is consumed and earned.

Revenue from exporting and government spending within the United States also pours into the income pool.

The pool not only has sources of new money, but it has drains too. What flows out of the income pool is money that's saved or invested in assets. In other words, it's organic wealth creation. Also, the money paid in taxes, spent on imports and used for loan repayments are drained out of the income pool.

Since income earned ultimately becomes consumed, only those who fill up their buckets create wealth. It may be easier for those with larger incomes to fill up their buckets, but anyone, even with a modest income, has some bucket they can use to start filling. Over time, the amount rescued from the income pool can be significant.

The ability to fill up buckets of income to create organic wealth is what motivates people to earn the most income possible. Asset appreciation is an excellent way to build wealth, of course, but to purchase an asset that appreciates will usually take using saved income. People, therefore, have the incentive to seek high-paying jobs, to become an entrepreneur or just work side gigs to supplement their existing income.

Wealth Creators Drain the Pool

Acting on the incentive to fill one's bucket, consequently, will result in the income pool draining and losing volume. Remember if someone consumes their income, it becomes income to another person and remains in the pool. But a saver removes income from the pool altogether. If the pool is drained from savers, then theoretically, there would be less money available for others to earn. This is exactly what those who say there's a wealth gap want people to believe.

The left decry the income gap between the rich and the poor. Buy why? If they understood free market capitalism, then they would know just because one person earns a high income, it doesn't take away the potential for someone else to earn a high income as well. For as long as a person or business meets market demand, income will be created. The ability to earn income by met demand is true regardless if there are many others scooping up buckets out of the income pool.

When people use their buckets to remove money from the income pool to create wealth, it doesn't mean there's less for everyone else. This is because new money is continually flowing into the income pool all the time. The money comes from government spending, exporting, investment capital, consumer debt, business loans and the consumption of assets.

Government Spending

Taxes are collected by government agencies. This could be property, sales, income, capital gains or another method of collection. The government removes money from the income pool more than any private business or person, but even so, it pours right back in the pool because of government spending. The exception is federal revenue consumed outside the United States.

International Trade

When U.S. firms sell products around the world, the money from those other economies gushes into our income pool. This revenue is different from what's received from sales within the U.S. because it's adding money to the income/consumption cycle. The opposite is also true, importing drains money from the income pool.

Investment Capital

Private equity firms and individual investors transfer billions of dollars into privately held companies. Much of this capital comes from income, which was once in the pool but was taken out and saved. These investments not only go for expenditures but also to pay workers. Once consumed, this flood of money comes pouring back into the income pool.

Think about the well-known ride sharing startups, Lyft and Uber. These companies received billions of dollars in private equity before going public, which was once outside the income pool. The billions in capital were used to grow these companies so now they have nearly a worldwide market reach. Most of this money was consumed and became income to drivers, employees and other vendors all to enter the pool once again.

As this investment capital gets consumed, it enters the income/consumption cycle to be swooshed about ever changing hands between consumption and income. As long as private equity is looking for a return, the capital will be invested in companies that are meeting market demand and therefore, re-enter the pool.

Consumer Debt and Business Loans

Every time someone takes out a loan, money surges back into the income pool. People borrow money for car loans/leases, credit card purchases, student loans, home mortgages and for other reasons. All this borrowing puts capital, which was outside of the pool, back into the income / consumption cycle.

Furthermore, businesses borrow from financial institutions to fund their businesses. This money is also consumed in our economy and becomes income for others. The income pool as a result gets fuller.

Consumption of Assets

Besides debt, the pool rises whenever assets are monetized such as when people retire, when estates are liquidated or just because of difficult economic situations. The money raised from the sale of the assets, if not reinvested, flows back into the income pool.

The bottom line is that when there are many people who are able to create organic wealth because they have high incomes, it doesn't prevent anyone else from earning an income and creating wealth as well.

The richest in our society can earn hundreds of thousands or even millions per year and it wouldn't prevent others from earning income by meeting demand. This makes the wealth gap or income gap between the rich and poor bridgeable. It just takes meeting market demand to earn income and then saving a portion to build wealth. The focus shouldn't be on halting the financial success of some people because this does nothing to increase the income of others.

Our focus as a society should be on helping people meet market demand with job growth policies, higher education and skills training. Moving people up the economic ladder ought to be the goal, not knocking people down.

What is Possible?

In order to visualize the benefits of lessening spending to invest for the future, we first need to know what's possible. Even someone with modest means can amass a small fortune over time. The secret ingredient is their income. The paycheck we work so hard for has the potential to be future wealth. It has great energy stored inside, which if spent right away, will be a small bang. On the other hand, the stored energy, if invested, can result in a future explosion.

What is your family's legacy regarding finances? Are you all investors, debt accumulators, over spenders? Every parent should teach their children from an early age to begin saving 10% to 20% of their income. It should be a habit we learn before adulthood because starting off with the right plan in place will allow for a massive accumulation of wealth over time.

If you're an adult and don't save, it's not too late. A reorder of your finances and perhaps downsizing a bit to begin this saving habit is still possible. Creating a budget and saving money each month is essential to your wealth building plan. Investing in an IRA, for example, is one easy way to create wealth over time. Contact a professional financial advisor to begin.

Let's take a look now at some numbers. If someone saves $500 per month from the age of 30 to when they retire at 65, at a conservative annual return rate of 7% from equities, the amount they would end up with would be over $856,000. This assumes they utilize a very passive *buy and hold strategy*. Buying and holding means never trying to time the market, but just keep investing no matter the direction of the stock market.

If the return is 10%, which is more in line with historical averages, it will amount to $1,699,423. If they started saving at age 45 for only twenty years, the amount at their retirement would be over $254,000 (7%). Can you imagine if everyone within our society began saving 10% to 20% from when they were teenagers? Teach your kids while they're young.

How much will you need to retire? Search online, there are many good retirement calculators to help you plan. If you're not on the right track and want to change your forecast, put in place what you learned in *Wealth Accumulation* from the last chapter. Creating more organic wealth and front-loading will help get you there.

Saving your income, instead of consuming its entirety, creates significant wealth over time. Several hundred thousand, or more, will allow you to retire young enough to enjoy it. It will also begin a legacy in your family to create wealth and then to pass along some of it to the next generation.

Not only will you increase your standard of living at retirement, but other savings can potentially be used for even more wealth creation. Maybe you see a great deal on a fixer upper and buy the house to flip. Because you have the resources available, the successful flip then increases your wealth further. Building wealth opens the door to new opportunities that would otherwise not exist.

Unlimited Millionaires

If wealth can be made into existence by anyone with an income, how many millionaires can there be in our economy? Theoretically, the answer is an unlimited number.

A millionaire, obviously, is someone with a net worth of at least one million dollars. These are people who created that wealth without taking it from someone else in some kind of wealth transfer. Most often, it was originally unconsumed income, which was earned in equal transactions by meeting demand from either a business venture or from employment income.

To help prove there can be unlimited millionaires in our economy, consider this hypothetical scenario. Let's say every employee began saving from the time they entered the workforce and continued to do so throughout their careers. If every wage earner in our economy began saving 10% to 20% of their income, is it possible most would be millionaires once they reached retirement age?

Do the math; most people would be filthy rich. For example, saving $400 per month for 40 years would result in $2.3 million. This assumes a 10% average return and a buy and hold strategy. If people saved and invested like this, then a majority of people would be millionaires by the time they retire.

People who forgo college and vocational education can become millionaires too even if their wage is less than the national average. Here's a fictitious scenario of a guy named James who starts working soon after high school. He'll just need to save $200 per month to reach a million at retirement, which is very doable by being intentional with a plan in place.

By utilizing a buy and hold strategy, after 50 years of investing $200 per month at only 7%, James would have $1.0 million. With a 10% return, he would have $3.0 million. If he saved $200/month for only 40 years at 10%, he would have $1.1 million.

Even if $1 million won't have the same buying power in forty years because of inflation, James can increase his $200 per month saving plan as his income rises due to the dollar devaluing. By having the same level of saving and investing in relation to his income, it will result in nearly the same buying power as a million dollars would have today.

These possible results are just from unconsumed employee income invested in an IRA or 401K and doesn't include any form of entrepreneurship or alternative investments. These hypotheticals just confirm a free people living within a free market are able to create substantial amounts of wealth by just using their saved income and very passive investments.

Buying Assets

Advocating for consumption, while at the same time advocating for saving, appears to be contradictory. There needs to be consumption for there to be both new income and a growing economy. But if people are saving income to build wealth, then theoretically, consumption would decline and new income wouldn't be created. This then would be harmful to the economy.

The answer to this dichotomy is twofold. First, if the people creating organic wealth buy assets with their savings, then the recipients would receive new income in an equal transaction. The saver receives a new asset and the seller receives new income, which they could consume in our economy. The income / consumption cycle would then continue.

Many sellers of assets, however, just buy other assets and don't consume their proceeds. While this is true, even if they do buy other assets, it would become income to someone else, who could consume it in the economy.

As an example, if Desiree buys a rental property from Sarah, then Sarah would have new income she could consume in the economy. If Sarah instead buys another property from Nicolas, then he could consume the income. This can go on and on until the money is eventually consumed by someone.

The difference between purchasing an asset and buying other things is the item's ability to store value. Assets have the ability to hold value or to even increase in value over time. Still other assets may even provide ongoing income. These are called productive assets. In contrast, what's received from consumption loses its value right away or it depreciates over time.

Here are some examples of assets that can be purchased with saved income: stocks, bonds, mineral rights, real estate, art, premium domain names, shares of peer-to-peer loans, intellectual property rights that pay royalties, gold, cryptocurrencies, antiques and NFT collectibles.

There is a second reason advocating for both consumption and saving isn't contradictory. Purchasing assets with saved income only delays income's consumption until a future time when the assets are monetized. Because assets are usually sold at some point, the saved income would eventually be consumed by the saver; just not right away.

Delayed Consumption

When people begin saving income for the purpose of buying assets, the amount that would have been consumed isn't gone forever. It's only delayed until a future time when the assets owned are sold to create income again. Most of the time asset sales occur at retirement for economic necessity or when an estate is liquidated. The selling of assets to raise cash for consumption will benefit that future economy.

Is it better for the economy to consume now or in the future? Neither is better because consuming immediately would be good for today's economy while consuming in the future would be good for a later economy. Over time, however, assets can appreciate substantially which allows for more consumption in the future.

When people begin saving to create wealth instead of consuming, it all works out in the end. Let's say Benjamin has been saving for the past thirty years while he worked at various jobs. When he enters retirement and begins consuming what he's saved, it will benefit that future economy. At the same time Ben retires, someone else begins saving. What's not consumed by the new saver is offset by the retiree, Ben, who is now monetizing his assets.

The takeaway here is that saving income to buy assets only delays consumption. In addition, the sellers of the assets receive income, which they could consume. Overall, our economy still benefits even when people create organic wealth with their saved income.

Saving Out of Fear

In uncertain economic times, the prudent pause consumption as much as possible out of fear of potential job loss. Instead of spending, these people will use their income to build up an emergency fund or to reduce any outstanding debt just in case there's a period of unemployment. This type of saving, however, just furthers the economic slowdown because it suspends, even if temporarily, the income generation cycle. There may be some asset purchases that create income for others, but mostly just cash savings or debt reduction.

So what may have been a $50 night out at a restaurant turns out to be a Ragu spaghetti dinner at home. The restaurant loses out on $50 of income which they could use to pay their employees. When many people stop eating out at the same time, restaurant workers get laid off. The COVID lockdowns obviously illustrated this better than any other recession we've experienced.

When the economy is humming along, savings deposited at the bank would be lent out to others who would use it in the consumption/income cycle. In a bad economy, however, if people aren't borrowing or lenders are not lending, then the money is not used to generate new income through the consumption of a loan.

In the next chapter, we'll see what private business and government should do in response to a recession or a demand shortfall. Essentially, though, the response should be to lower employee wages and product prices to prevent high unemployment. Even though wages are lowered, product prices also decline, which makes the purchasing power from the lower income the same as it was previously for those products and services where prices have declined.

Despite the fact saving out of fear isn't ideal for the income generation cycle, it's still beneficial for the saver in two ways. Any debt reduction is always good because it lessens risk. Secondly, as debt gets paid off, it frees up monthly income available for consumption and savings.

Unfortunately though, this type of saving out of fear of job loss may not actually result in wealth accumulation. Without having an intentional wealth building plan, the purpose of the emergency fund savings or the debt reduction was just to alleviate possible future economic hardship. When the fear subsides, and the economy improves, the saving plan turns out to be just pent-up consumption.

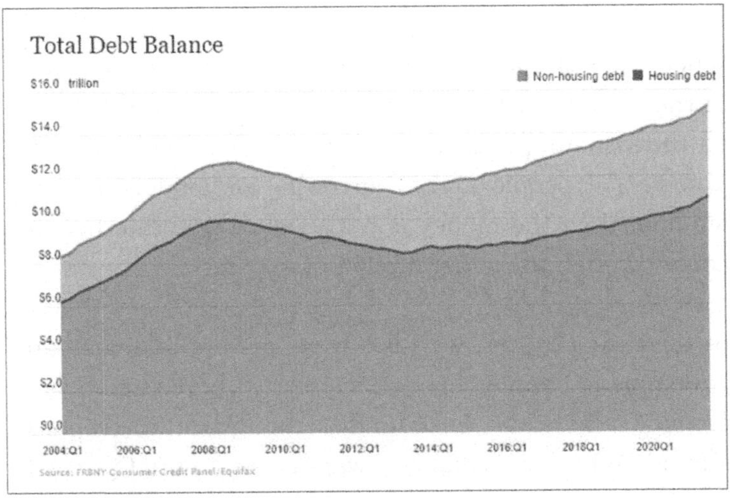

The recession of 2008 and the following recovery illustrate this. As you can see from the above chart,[8] because of the recession in 2008, total debt changed course and declined. But as the economy began improving after

2012, total debt rose higher once again. Through the third quarter of 2021, U.S. household debt increased to a record of $15.24 trillion.

Total Debt Balance in the previous chart represents U.S. household debt that includes both housing and non-housing debt. Housing debt includes mortgage balances and home equity lines of credit. Non-housing debt includes auto loans, credit card debt and student loans.

Buying assets is an important next step in building wealth. These purchases exchange saved income for assets that can appreciate or provide ongoing income.

The ability for our economy to create unlimited wealth is only possible because of our market-oriented economic system of capitalism. Without the freedom to supply something to a marketplace that's demanded by others, new income couldn't be earned. Not having earned income leaves people on the sidelines without the power to consume or to build organic wealth.

- FOUR -

Effective Supply

Organic wealth flourishes in free market capitalism because it's an environment where society has the liberty to engage in economic activity. The Gross Domestic Product (GDP) will have robust growth and reach its *potential* when there are many equal transactions occurring where people are pursuing income by meeting market demand. The more freedom a society possesses to enter a marketplace to earn income, the more wealth that will be created.

This truth that *freedom creates wealth* is also fundamental to the theory of supply side economics. The proposition of supply side theory is the government's policies toward businesses and wage earners (supply) should allow them to be as free as possible to meet demand. This is the true purpose of supply side proponents.

Some good examples of supply side policies would be low corporate tax rates, as few regulations as possible, education and job training that fill market needs, eliminating illegal immigrant hiring, fair trade agreements with other nations, and merit and market needs based legal immigration reforms.

Any policy making it easier for people and businesses to meet market demand will allow an economy to grow stronger. A growing economy, of course, has many benefits such as job openings for every demographic, career and entrepreneurial opportunities, upward mobility, higher wages and an abundance of available investments to build wealth.

These benefits should be the goal of our economic system. Otherwise, what's the point? If we allow our jobs for most industries to be replaced by automation, artificial intelligence and outsourcing, then we'll end up in a downward spiral of declining economic output. If jobs are gone, then people won't have the money to buy the products and services businesses produce. Taking it to its logical end, such a demand shortfall would eventually spell the end of business.

The direction of our policies, therefore, needs to be all encompassing with jobs in mind. What I mean by that is we need policies that give freedom to both businesses and wage earners. What the entirety of supply needs is the liberty to enter a market to earn as much income as possible by meeting demand.

It may be surprising wage earners are included within supply side economics. The reason is that they meet demand in the employment market. Employers demand workers with the necessary skills to meet the employer's needs. Therefore, wage earners are included in supply. Not to be confused, they are also a part of demand.

When employees exchange their labor for income, they are part of supply. When they consume that income, then they're counted on the demand side. The same is true of businesses. When businesses bring products and services to market, they are on the supply side. When they're paying employees and vendors, then they are on the demand side.

Supply side policies should ultimately be a win for both wage earners and business because they each make up supply. This is the only way to reach society's objectives of economic opportunity for everyone and economic growth. There is a conflict, however, between these objectives and the interests of multinational corporations.

Over the last several decades of globalization, being *pro-business* has come to include the interests of global corporations. But we need to rethink that notion because many times those interests conflict with the goals for our economy. Being pro-business should only be a supply side stance benefiting the entire supply, which includes the supply of wage earners residing in the United States.

For instance, having a business environment resulting in U.S. based companies moving operations to another country to reduce labor costs is counterproductive to society's aim for a strong labor market. Some may say it's an example of supply side economics because paying less on labor allows these businesses to compete. Thus, they would argue, offshoring helps companies meet demand. The easily identifiable problem is it harms the labor supply within the U.S.

This belief, any policy benefiting big business is good is not necessarily true. If our business environment harms the supply of wage earners, then we don't have effective supply side policies. A simple test should be a cause-and-effect question. When considering a supply side policy that benefits businesses, what would be the effect on the supply of labor?

If it doesn't benefit the supply of labor but rather, harms that supply, then the policy doesn't align itself with society's desire for a dynamic and healthy job market. A better solution to counteract offshoring is asking how we could enact policies allowing American businesses to stay here and still compete.

The corporate tax reform of 2018 reduced the corporate tax rate from 35% to 21% and was changed from a worldwide tax system to territorial,[1] which means revenue earned in a foreign market won't be taxed again by the U.S. This reduction in taxes doesn't lessen a company's labor costs, but it does lower their overall expenses and potentially allows them to stay operating in the U.S.

Is a lower corporate tax rate enough? Possibly not for labor intensive companies so other supply side changes may have to be required. Whatever the new policy changes are, more freedom to meet demand should be the goal for the entirety of supply.

Let's consider the practice of hiring illegal immigrants. Certain industries benefit by hiring illegals because they can pay them low wages. These companies save substantially on wage expense so it does help them compete. It's not a good supply side policy to turn a blind eye to this practice, however, because it harms the supply of legal workers. First, it takes positions away the legal workforce could otherwise fill; second, it puts downward pressure on their wages.

By requiring only the hiring of citizens and legal visa holders, it would immediately increase the labor expense of these companies. They would have to follow minimum wage laws and more importantly, become subject to the legal employment market, which ultimately determines the proper wage levels.

If product prices increase as a result, then the consumer will have to pay more. If raising prices on products won't work because of foreign competition, then other supply side policies should be considered so American firms can compete. Some ideas would be to lower the corporate tax rate further or insisting on fair trade agreements with countries that have inherent trade advantages such as low wages, little regulations and where shipping into the U.S. isn't prohibitive.

Free trade would be ideal, but the reality is a wealthy country like the United States should only enter fair trade agreements especially with developing nations. Fair trade is an attempt to level the playing field. This could require one nation to step up their environmental laws, workforce compensation and removal of trade barriers. It may also include tariffs, not as a barrier, but to offset the competitive advantage a manufacturer or farmer has in a developing nation over U.S. based companies.

What, You Don't Say?

Supply side economics isn't a phenomenon beginning with Art Laffer, Dick Cheney and a napkin. Art's famous curve illustrates how lowering taxes in the prohibitive range will increase revenue to the government.[2] The Laffer Curve was adopted by President Ronald Reagan (R) and was the basis for the Reagan tax cuts of the 1980s. To the left's chagrin, revenues to the U.S. Treasury almost doubled over Reagan's eight years in office.

Many historical revisionists from the left deceive their audience by saying his tax cuts caused massive budget deficits. The truth is, as revenues went up, government spending went up further. Tax cuts didn't cause budget deficits; spending money like there was no tomorrow did.

The Washington Post too denies Reagan's tax policy's success by not using actual revenue to the Treasury as the number to determine if revenues went up.[3] Instead, they claim revenue as a percent of GDP is the best way to compare between years. They then tell their readers the percentage declined over Reagan's two terms. Thus, his tax policy didn't increase revenue to the government.

But, consumer of WaPo, this is wrong. If tax rates are cut, then any growth in GDP will outpace the growth rate of tax revenue. That's just plain logic. The fact is GDP increased because of Reagan's tax policies resulting in more revenues even if the revenue as a percentage of GDP declined.

The Laffer Curve is an example of a supply side policy Republicans have become known for, but it's not the definition of supply side economics. Even before there was a Republican Party, which began in 1854 to oppose slavery,[4] there was a supply side advocate as far back as our country's founding.

Jean-Baptiste Say was a French classical economist and was one of the world's first supply side economists. Say wrote a letter to Thomas Jefferson in November 1803[5] and provided him a copy of his newly published book, *Treatise on Political Economy.*[6] Jefferson wrote back to J. B. Say acknowledging he received it, but it wasn't until years later we learn of Jefferson's view of his work.

Say wrote to Jefferson again about possibly immigrating to the United States because of the turmoil in France caused by Napoleon Bonaparte writing, "the need to breathe the air of a free country, while harboring no hope that France will become well administered."[7]

In March 1815, Jefferson replied to Say and wrote, "I had considered it (Treatise on Political Economy) in it's (sic) first form as superceding (sic) all other works on that subject."[8] That was quite the compliment at the time considering *The Wealth of Nations* (1776) by Adam Smith greatly influenced Jefferson and the Founding Fathers.

Say's theories informed his readers how wealth was created, which contradicted the mercantilist's view that saw wealth as zero sum. Mercantilists believed wealth could only be accumulated and distributed from a finite source. Therefore, that view hindered international trade.

Many credit Say with the notion *utility* determines product pricing.[9] Classical economic thought until then believed production costs determined what the consumer price would be. Say argued perceived value is what ultimately determines price.[10]

From this concept, he believed all markets would eventually clear. Meaning, if product remained unsold, a supplier would lower prices to move the inventory. By lowering the price, demand would increase. As far as gluts, which are overproduction of goods where there's not enough demand, clearing markets would eventually alleviate any glut.

We can see the effects of clearing markets from the 1920 depression. After WWI ended in November 1918, millions of troops were returning home looking for work. This was a shock to the economy. On top of high unemployment, consumer inflation was rising sharply: 17% and 15% from 1917 to 1920.[11] The federal budget too had increased substantially due to costs from fighting in the European conflict. The government's response was to let the market correct itself.

Instead of goosing the economy with government spending and cheap money, which is what we do now, the federal budget was cut over the next four years from $18.5 billion in 1919 to $3.3 billion in 1922,[12] an 82% reduction. Instead of cutting rates, the Federal Reserve raised them from 4.56% in October 1919 to a record high of 7% in June 1920.[13] The Fed didn't raise rates to stem the tide of inflation, but to guard their 40% gold reserve ratio to liabilities. Gold had been fleeing the country in 1919 as a result of the end of the gold export embargo.[14]

The result was 10.9% deflation[15] and an unemployment rate of 11.9% (estimate) in 1921.[16] The market was clearing itself of excess goods and bad capital allocations. Businesses that weren't solvent went bankrupt instead of being propped up with easy money. Wage levels, which were stagnant, began to decline as prices fell. What looked harsh and merciless turned out to be short lived. The economy rebounded as investment went to companies well-run and meeting demand. The depression that ushered in the 1920s, caused by market distortions resulting from WWI, lasted only a year and a half. By 1923, the unemployment rate was 3.2% (estimate) and the Roaring Twenties was well underway.

Entrepreneurs

Say also coined the term, *entrepreneur,*[17] which if you read an English translation of his treatise uses the word *adventurer* since a word for entrepreneur didn't exist. The concept an entrepreneur is a special talent wasn't distinguishable in Adam Smith's Wealth of Nations.

Say considered the entrepreneur the fourth factor of production. An entrepreneur has to utilize the other three factors (land, labor and capital) against market risk and profit potential to produce products having demand.

Consider a socialist system, which eliminates entrepreneur talents. Let's suppose the government tells a footwear firm to produce shoes for the public. The results are shoes without much variety, and possibly disliked by everyone. In contrast, an entrepreneur would first learn what different kinds of shoes consumers' desire, and then he figures out a way to produce them at a price where they will sell for a profit.

Only the talents of entrepreneurs can develop products at the right price satisfying consumer wants. Not only are entrepreneurial talents found in small startups, but big tech companies have harnessed entrepreneur abilities to adapt and diversify their product offerings.

We see this just by looking at some of the largest companies in the U.S.: Amazon, Apple, Microsoft and Google. Are these companies run with a traditional hierarchy reacting slowly to market changes or are they still on the cutting edge of future trends? They're on the cutting edge because they're utilizing entrepreneur talents within their organizations.

Say's Law of Markets

Jean-Baptiste Say's most well-known contribution to the study of economics has become known as Say's Law of

Markets or simply, Say's Law. This law was summarized by John Maynard Keynes as *supply creates its own demand.* While this could be an accurate summary, you may get the wrong meaning at first glance. It doesn't mean creating a supply of something will magically be met with demand from enough willing buyers. This summary of Say's Law is how Keynes discredited what Say believed, but his surmising was misleading.

Say actually didn't call his teaching a *law*. He did, however, write that supplying something opens the door for the supplier to demand other products. Those other products then have a larger market. He wrote in chapter XV of his book, *A Treatise on Political Economy*, "Thus, the mere circumstance of the creation of one product immediately opens a vent for other products."

We'll take Keynes at his own words from his book, *The General Theory of Employment, Interest and Money (1936)*, where he reveals his misinterpretation of *supply creates its own demand* several times:

1. John Keynes claimed that Say's Law meant the entire costs from the supply side must be met by the demand side: "The whole of the costs of production must necessarily be spent (by demand) in the aggregate, directly or indirectly, on purchasing the product."[18]
2. He asserted at any level of production, the supply price will be met by demand: "The aggregate demand price is equal to the aggregate supply price for all levels of output and employment."[19]

3. "(Supply creates its own demand) must mean that $f(N)$ (demand function) and $\phi(N)$ (supply function) are equal for all values of N (persons employed)."[20] Interpretation: The workers required to produce for actual demand are equal to the workers in total production at all employment levels. In other words, you can't out produce demand.

If Keynes's definition of Say's Law was correct, then J. B. Say wouldn't have believed utility was the ultimate determination of price, and that markets would eventually clear by lowering the price. The buyers, according to Keynes' understanding, would just buy at whatever price. Or would Say have believed entrepreneurs were a special talent; all that would be necessary is to produce something and it would sell.

Also, if Keynes was right about classical economists, then adherents wouldn't believe gluts or overproduction could exist. But according to J. B. Say, producing more than demand warrants and declining income on the demand side were the reasons for gluts:

> The glut of a particular commodity arises from its having outrun the total demand for it in one or two ways; either because it has been produced in excessive abundance, or because the production of other commodities has fallen short. It is because the production of some commodities has declined, that other commodities are superabundant. To use a more hackneyed phrase, people have bought less, because they have made less profit.[21]

The fact is Keynes wrongfully defined Say's Law to make people believe the law meant the very acts of production were all that were necessary to have a healthy economy with full employment. He must have thought the world was really stupid before he came along. Say's Law was not an antiquated belief from the unenlightened past that needed replacement by the light of Keynes.

When we break down Say's Law, the true meaning becomes apparent. *Supply creates its own demand* simply means one has to produce something in order to demand something. Woops, I did it too. Let me clearly explain this so I'm not accused of believing in hocus pocus. Someone has to produce value for a market where it will sell to willing buyers. With their sale proceeds, they can demand other products. If a product doesn't sell, then there'll be no sale proceeds and no ability to demand.

The truth of Say's Law turns idle people into productive people. The money earned by supplying something, in turn, creates an equal value of demand for something else. That something else can be products, services or investments. Additionally, it can remain as money, which represents future demand for products or investments. As Say said:

> Even when money is obtained with a view to hoard or bury it, the ultimate object is always to employ it in a purchase of some kind. The heir of the lucky finder uses it in that way, if the miser do not; for money, as money, has no other use than to buy with.[22]

For an example of Say's Law, take a worker who supplies labor for a company. In return for their production, the employer pays the worker income. When the employee receives their paycheck, they can then demand other products of the same value, which increases the market size for those products. This is Say's Law in action.

What Say said is what I've been saying so far. In order to create income, you have to meet market demand first. When demand is met, income is earned. This income gives the person the power to demand other products (consumption) or investments (organic wealth) of equal value to what was earned.

If you study Say's Law, you come to the conclusion the emphasis should be on supplying something of value that satisfies market demand. Because once this is accomplished, the earned income will allow the demand of other products or investments in a marketplace. By having this emphasis in free market capitalism is what results in organic wealth creation.

Say was a supply sider. He believed governments should mostly not interfere with commerce. Even so, he believed they should stimulate production, which is having an economy where people are encouraged to produce products valued by others. Governments encouraging consumption to stimulate the economy have it backwards according to Jean-Baptiste:

> The encouragement of mere consumption is no benefit to commerce; for the difficulty lies in sup-

> plying the means, not in stimulating the desire of consumption; and we have seen that production alone furnishes those means. Thus, it is the aim of good government to stimulate production, of bad government to encourage consumption.[23]

Production that meets demand is the work of entrepreneurs who must determine if a product can be produced having utility at an agreeable price. Good government policy should be enacted making it as easy as possible for producers to enter the marketplace. Facilitating commerce, not obstructing it, is good government policy.

Essentially, consumption doesn't need stimulating by the government apart from improving consumer confidence. Policies encouraging consumption won't produce much growth or wealth because the emphasis isn't for supply to satisfy demand, but just to expand the demand side. Expanding the demand side usually involves harming supply with higher taxes, smothering regulations, and diverting otherwise productive capital to Treasury bonds so the government can consume more. This is ineffective and the opposite of what leads to growth.

Ineffective Demand

As mentioned already, Say's Law was assailed by John Maynard Keynes in his book, which was published in the midst of the Great Depression where the unemployment rate peaked at nearly 25%. But Keynes wasn't the first Keynesian. Many of the policies Keynes would come to advocate had already been implemented. Following the

1929 stock market crash, President Herbert Hoover (R) cut income taxes by $160 million to increase aggregate demand.[24] The Federal Reserve too began slashing the discount rate for the next two years from 6% until it reached 1.5% in 1931.[25]

To further the increase of aggregate demand, Hoover signed government spending bills, which included public works projects swelling the national deficit.[26] He even built a dam. In his attempt to close the gap in the budget, Hoover increased taxes substantially in 1932.[27] The top rate went from 25% to 63%, but even so, tax receipts stayed the same in 1933. Increasing taxation just removes what would be productive capital over to consumption, thereby, preventing future expansion.

President Hoover also intervened in the economy by not allowing markets to clear. His meddling involved farm loans to maintain agriculture prices.[28] He also had protectionist trade barriers so consumers would buy American-made products to bolster prices. But foreign governments retaliated and prevented U.S. exports. Global trade fell by 2/3 and further contributed to the worldwide downturn.[29]

Soon after the 1929 stock market crash, Hoover encouraged business leaders across the country to not lower wages in response to the slumping economy.[30] He wanted wages to remain high and for profits to decline instead. Hoover believed high wages is what leads to prosperity. But this is the opposite of what needs to occur in a downturn within a free market. Prices should naturally fall as supply entices the new lower level of demand until it becomes balanced again. In order to lower prices, businesses need to lower their costs, which include their largest expense of labor.

A free market that can adjust prices and wages will prevent large scale unemployment. Hoover's policies didn't prevent unemployment, but accelerated it. As prices fell, the only alternative for businesses was to lay people off since they committed to not lower wages at the behest of President Hoover.

Not long after taking office in 1933, President Franklin Delano Roosevelt (D) continued down the same path of increasing aggregate demand at the expense of the supply side. The New Deal policies suffocated businesses with heavy regulations and high taxation, which only lessened investment and production.

Roosevelt also believed the *high prices and wages leads to prosperity* theory started by Hoover. FDR intervened in the economy with his New Deal policies aimed to curtail production, artificially raising prices. This made food and other products much more difficult to afford, which added to the suffering of the millions struggling in the depression. These policies were the reverse of what the market needed to rebalance.

A 2004 article published in the Journal of Political Economy,[31] *New Deal Policies and the Persistence of the Great Depression: A General Equilibrium Analysis* concluded FDR's policies prolonged the Great Depression by seven years. The study's co-author, economist Lee Ohanian said, "High wages and high prices in an economic slump run contrary to everything we know about market forces in economic downturns. As we've seen in the past several years, salaries and prices fall when unemployment is high. By artificially inflating both, the New Deal policies short-circuited the market's self-correcting forces."

The end of the Great Depression is often attributed to World War II. But while sending millions away to fight in the war may have helped unemployment, the inflated GDP many cite was because of government war spending. Domestic prosperity hadn't yet returned to the country, however. The components of GDP tell the real story:[32]

	GDP	C	Inv	Exp	Gov
1941	126.7	64.0%	14.3%	0.8%	20.9%
1942	161.8	55.0%	6.4%	-0.2%	38.8%
1943	198.6	50.3%	3.1%	-1.1%	47.7%
1944	219.8	49.5%	3.5%	-0.9%	47.9%
1945	223.0	53.8%	4.8%	-0.4%	41.7%
1946	222.2	64.9%	14.0%	3.2%	17.8%

Pearl Harbor was attacked on December 7, 1941. The next day the U.S. declared war on Japan and entered WWII.

The previous table shows GDP for the year was $126.7 billion, which was made up of 64.0% personal consumption (C), 14.3% private investment (Inv), .8% net exports (Exp) and 20.9% total government spending (Gov).

For the years of WWII (1942 - 1945), government spending increased substantially. This is the component of GDP causing GDP's rise. During the same period, however, private investment declined dramatically and likewise personal consumption. Net exports also took a dive. This tells us it was only government spending that increased GDP and not a growing private sector economy.

It wasn't until after the war that the economy truly begins to grow. Federal government spending was $84 billion in 1945, but in 1946, federal spending had dropped by 65.7% to $28.8 billion! The cuts in government spending allowed the private sector to use its capital to expand in search of revenues. These cuts in spending and the unwinding of many of the New Deal policies is what brought prosperity back and decidedly ended the Great Depression.[33]

There's a stark contrast between the depressions of 1920 and 1929. The depression of 1929 turned into the Great Depression of which its effects lingered until the close of WWII, compared to its predecessor of 18 months. It's not difficult to see the reason it lasted so long was because of government meddling. Had the first Keynesians allowed the market to correct itself, the depression may have been as short lived as the one at the beginning of the decade and there'd be no reason to call it Great.

Keynes Blame Game

Keynes discredited Say's Law in the minds of the public and government officials by using his misinterpretation of its meaning. If supply creates its own demand, then there wouldn't be such a demand shortfall as seen in the Great Depression. So Keynes blamed the depression and its high unemployment on classical economic thought. This then allowed him to introduce his theory about demand side economics. What Keynes got wrong, as stated, was Say's Law applies to production that meets demand, not just willy-nilly production.

The cause of the Great Depression is debated, but it certainly wasn't the result of classical economic practices or beliefs. Say's Law didn't instruct the Federal Reserve to inflate the economy with easy money during the boom of the 1920s.[34] The Fed's actions artificially propelled the stock market attracting personal savings and business profits, which poured in until the Fed decided to put the brakes on. Then the jig was up. The resulting economic shocks from the stock market crash of 1929, bank failures and interventionist government policies devastated consumer and business confidence and would have still occurred had Keynes been king.

Principle of Effective Demand

It's said Keynes believed the opposite of Say that demand creates supply or that demand ultimately equals supply (D = S). Keynes observed the problem was there weren't enough buyers to incentivize firms to increase production and employment. So, to have full employment, the supply side would need adequate demand.

In his book, Keynes propositioned the principle he called *effective demand.* This is the point where aggregate demand and aggregate supply become equal. Consequently, businesses won't produce more goods because buyers at this point are at its maximum. Those who are unemployed wouldn't be able to find jobs because the supply side doesn't have a need to hire.

At this hypothetical place of effective demand, he believed governments should cut personal taxes (not a bad thing) or spend more money to increase aggregate demand. This would theoretically move unsold inventory and entice firms to invest more capital to increase the supply, which would increase employment.

This principle of increasing aggregate demand depends on the belief that demand would be satisfied at this equilibrium point, and supply wouldn't be seeking to meet demand any further. I don't believe, however, those assumptions can be made.

In reality, supply is continually attempting to satisfy demand especially in unregulated environments. Demand will never be completely satisfied because of competition, innovation and invention. A start-up with a better product will compete for existing market share by deploying new capital. Thus, employment rises. Or an existing business with a new product will compete for the buying power of demand. Again, employment increases.

In a free market economy, entrepreneurs with the profit motive will always work to entice demand. When there's no barrier to enter a market, human nature will take over in the pursuit of earning income. Human nature and freedom are why effective demand is wrong.

Those on the sidelines are not dependent upon a satiated equilibrium between the supply of goods and national income or the buying power from the demand side. They just need to meet market demand. Today, job openings are easier than ever to identify because of the internet. These listings are by companies competing for income.

Let's illustrate a sidelined unemployed person named Eric within this theory of effective demand. Instead of hoping for a government shovel-ready job or a guaranteed government income, he sees the chance to do something entrepreneurial. So he goes out and cuts people's lawns in his neighborhood diverting people's disposable income to himself.

After doing so, he has income to consume in the economy, which provides for his needs and effectively replaces the consumption of those who paid him to cut their grass. Just from this one act of meeting demand, the national income increases.

To further expand on this, a household with long grass earned money from their job and would have spent $40 of it at Target. Instead, they find more utility in paying Eric $40 to cut their grass, which he uses to shop at Target. The store Target didn't lose anything, but Eric's income went from zero to $40 and the national income likewise increased by $40. Overtime, he gets a loan to buy equipment and hires people to cut even more lawns, which increases the national income further. The bottom line is employment improved because of meeting market demand not because of some government investment.

Let's say the market tells Eric he should accept credit cards, which he does with his smartphone and a Square Reader. So now people are getting lawns and other projects done on credit. The customers who are using credit are using more than their disposable income. Because Eric is meeting demand, the GDP, the national income, and employment are all increasing. So much for a satisfied equilibrium between supply and demand.

Eric's business is an example against effective demand and the need for government investment spending to create jobs. What creates jobs is less government, private property protections, low taxes and free markets where all the participants are incentivized to earn as much income as possible.

Demand Shortfall

The way Keynes saw the world, aggregate demand would steadily decline in capitalism because people hold money. In addition to hoarding money, government spending outside the country and trade deficits would cause the buying power to decline. By not using all this capital to demand products within the U.S., it would cause a demand shortfall. This basically means the demand for products, services, investments, and labor would be less than 100% of what was earned as income. A demand shortfall would cause declining economic growth and also high unemployment.

This isn't the story of our economy, though, because thus far, the free market capitalist system of the U.S. encourages economic growth. We don't rely upon a managed economy where bureaucrats determine national output. A free market-based economy leads to new businesses, capital investment, an educated workforce, new technologies, discoveries of raw materials, and so much more. All of this for the pursuit of meeting demand to earn income. As a result, our national output grows, productivity improves, employment increases, and the standard of living improves for everyone.

In addition, hoarding is offset by borrowing. Consumers use more than their income to make purchases. New money is added continually from credit card purchases, auto leases, student loans, home mortgages, business loans and other loans. This borrowing is from met demand. There's also new private capital used by startups and other businesses to pay vendors and to hire people.

All of these loans and the monetization of assets pump new income into our economy. This new income enlarges the amount of money in the *Circular Flow of Income.*[35] This is the business income received from the consumption of loans and liquidation of assets are used to pay workers who then buy products and services—then repeating over and over again.

Some may discount borrowing because loans have to be paid back. The idea being, the principal portion of the loan-repayments negates future demand for products, which neutralizes the benefit of the initial loan amount. If you make that case, then you have to allow for hoarding of cash to be eventually spent. People don't demand money as a commodity, but for bank deposits, debt reduction, investments and for future consumption.

The economic activity of producing to earn income makes up for any would be demand shortfall resulting from hoarding, sending money away to foreign countries or for any organic wealth creation. This is why a growing GDP is important. The GDP for a single term measures both output and national income within the country. If it grows compared to the previous term, it means aggregate demand (and supply) has increased. If GDP shrinks, it means aggregate demand has decreased and there's been a demand shortfall. A growing GDP is the final verdict for organic wealth creation. Those who save income do not harm economic growth and certainly do not cause a demand shortfall.

Demandocratic Party

The freer an economy, the more economic prosperity there will be. That's what conservatives believe. This isn't just a theory, but is evidentiary provable by looking at the free market capitalist system of the United States—the most prosperous nation in the world. This wealth didn't just appear even though we have an abundance of natural resources. The wealth which was created was by a free people who were incentivized to prosper because there weren't barriers to income creation. Anything is possible within a free economy when people are able to reap the rewards of risk taking or for hard work.

When conservatives characterize today's liberal economic proposals as being socialist, it's because these policies destroy existing wealth and the mechanisms for future wealth creation just like full-blown socialism. Additionally, these policies appear to be steps toward the goal of transforming the U.S. economy into actual socialism. Each step they take towards that goal is considered progress by progressives.

Progressive politicians have taken Keynes's theories and run with them. They're all about stimulating the demand side of the economy. They promise voters free things like a guaranteed job, healthcare and college, but this requires forcing other people to pay for it. Many Democrats have staked out positions constraining the supply side in order to stimulate the demand side; even though, supply side expansion is what leads to more employment. Most of their proposals when broken down can be characterized by the following equation:

$$I \Rightarrow D = S \propto E$$

Demand (D) equals supply (S) which results in a proportional level of employment (E). Government investments (I) on the demand side are supposed to increase the supply side, which theoretically would also proportionally increase employment.

This basic mathematical statement is why Democrats have no problem with policies harming supply. They are purely demand centric looking at just one side of the equation. If their agenda damages supply, then it means more demand stimulus would be needed. Regarding this equation, they truly are the party of the left.

Illegal Immigration

Consider Democratic policies that essentially encourage illegal immigration. Taking positions allowing for an undocumented workforce harms the supply side of legal labor. Jobs are taken away and it lowers wages.

Even so, undermining the labor supply doesn't faze them because their true motivation is turning illegal immigrants into Democratic voters. As a bonus, it doesn't negatively affect the demand side. The demand side is just fine because illegal immigrants "do the jobs Americans won't" and as a result, they become consumers in the economy. So the Democratic Party prospers at the expense of American citizens and the legal workforce.

$15 Minimum Wage

A new minimum wage that's higher than current local market rates stimulate demand and harms supply. This is because it artificially raises the costs to employers resulting in unequal transactions. Forced wages are not equal to the value received, so employers will reduce jobs in response and raise prices to cover the costs of the remaining employees. Even though the demand side is collecting higher wages, job losses and a more costly living may cancel out any demand stimulus.

Tax Increases

The left is promising to raise the corporate tax rates back to 35% from 21%, even though Biden proposed 28%. Tax increases doesn't help job creation, but it will allow them to raise revenue to stimulate demand for their programs. If the supply side is hurt by raising taxes, then more demand stimulus would be needed. They just have to apply the equation by investing in demand to increase the supply output in their attempt to raise employment.

Government Programs

Providing free things such as Medicare expansion, universal healthcare and college are demand side stimuli. Government funded healthcare and college may be a windfall for the medical and education industries, but it's definitely not free and will require taxing the supply side of the economy.

Most people recognize today's guaranteed student loans and health insurance have the effect of escalating costs because of unchecked demand. If the government began providing free college and healthcare for everyone, it would be a demand side stimulus on steroids resulting in a further escalation of prices. The problem is the producers would have to pay for the ever increasing costs with higher tax rates.

Climate Change

Progressives believe we only have ten to twelve years before fixing the climate is beyond repair. Besides raising taxes on business, imposing regulations for the climate's sake obviously harms the supply side. Over regulating the economy will result in fewer jobs, but that doesn't matter when considering the Demandocratic equation. It just means more demand stimulus would be required.

The left believes government can constrain supply side activity as much as is necessary with taxation and regulations to support their policy objectives. Doing so will require as much stimulus as would be necessary on demand to increase supply. They believe this will then lead to near full employment for those who want to work.

They also expect that business will always adapt to whatever the rules are and; therefore, high taxation or heavy regulations aren't a detriment to economic growth. The supply side will just adjust no matter what.

The origin of this demand stimulus philosophy can be traced back to the work of John Maynard Keynes. Ever since Keynes, governments around the world have been trying to stimulate demand at the cost of constraining the supply side.

The Obama Test

There was a great debate in 2018 on who deserved credit for the booming U.S. economy. The intellectually honest concluded Donald Trump does. Some were saying President Trump inherited a strong economy that began under Barack Obama. Even former President Obama himself pointed to his Administration's job numbers while he was on the campaign trail before the 2018 midterms. He said the good monthly job numbers under

Trump were just a continuation from his time in office adding we all should say, "Thanks, Obama."[36]

The markets didn't collapse and the economy didn't go into recession with Donald Trump's policies, as predicted by mainstream economists. Paul Krugman infamously stated the markets would "never recover" because of a President Trump and "we are very probably looking at a global recession, with no end in sight."[37] All these predictions were, of course, proven false. How could so many experts be so wrong? The answer lies within their cherished economic theory.

Keynesian economic policies are advocated and used by liberals to try to manage the U.S. economy. This is especially true whenever there's a looming recession. Under this theory, there will always be times of economic recessions and high unemployment with capitalism because product demand will eventually decline due to a demand shortfall. Keynesians contend suppliers cannot react fast enough to lower product prices and wages in response to declining demand so they lay people off. They essentially deny the ability for markets to clear on their own.

The solution, the theory advances, is government intervention with monetary and fiscal policy. The monetary policy is carried out by the Federal Reserve. The idea is for the Fed to lower interest rates to incentivize borrowing to stimulate demand. The fiscal policy is government investments (spending) on the demand side. This is paid with increased taxes on the supply side and borrowing, which both remove investment capital from the economy.

Under President Obama, we implemented Keynesian policies entirely. The interest rates were lowered to near zero, the Federal Reserve *printed* over four trillion dollars and the nation's debt nearly doubled to almost twenty trillion dollars because of the massive budget deficits.

The result of applying their equation, $I \Rightarrow D = S \propto E$, wasn't a success. Despite the entire demand stimulus, the economic recovery was still anemic resulting in unimproved employment during Obama's first term. In order to see their demand stimulus succeed, some liberal economists believed government spending should have been some multiple higher than the $trillions spent.

That failure to improve employment is why the left's control over Biden's policies had such massive stimulus. Not only did they rob America for political gain, but also the theory that massive multiple trillion dollar spending programs will reduce unemployment. The socialists, however, have ulterior motives than jobs. We'll delve into their plans beginning in chapter seven, *Democratic Socialism.*

We're supposed to take these people seriously that spending should have been much greater under Obama? That's a lot of stimulus in an *attempt* to move the needle on employment. I would like to point out inefficiency isn't very effective. It should also make the rest of us conclude increasing aggregate demand with massive government spending doesn't proportionally improve employment.

This should have been the lesson from Obama's presidency, but under the Biden-Harris regime, we'll have to suffer the same result again. Colossal spending, higher taxes and heavy regulations are the opposite of what's needed to have a robust economy.

The country didn't experience a job recovery during Obama's first term, which was from 2009 to 2012. The unemployment rate for January 2009 was 7.8% and it rose from there staying mostly above 9% for the first 33 months. The unemployment rate during that time peaked at 10%.[38] For the remainder of his first term, the unemployment rate improved modestly by about a percentage point to around 8%. The recession officially ended in June 2009, but the economy didn't snap back as would be expected based on historical recoveries.

It took until January 2016 for the unemployment rate to fall under 5%, which was where the rate was before the housing and financial crisis began. The drop in the unemployment rate was partly due to people leaving the labor force. The *participation rate* depicts the percentage of people who are currently employed and also those who are unemployed, but who're looking for work. This latter group is what the unemployment rate measures.

The participation rate dropped steadily from January 2009, where it stood at 65.7%, until bottoming in September 2015 at 62.4%.[39] The three point drop in the participation rate made the unemployment rate appear better than it otherwise would have. The labor force participation rate was moderately improving under President Trump until the pandemic blew everything up. The November 2021 rate was 61.8%.

The reason the economy didn't snap back was because of the policies coming out of the Obama Administration. The problem with their prescribed Keynesian medicine was it didn't do anything to improve business and consumer confidence but instead, exacerbated the concerns of the public.

The near zero interest rates, bank bailouts and the flood of easy money from the Central Bank didn't allow markets to clear. Prices and wages couldn't adjust so unemployment remained high. Additionally, there was a misallocation of private capital to prop up businesses that weren't solvent. The market, if free, will reward companies that are meeting demand with investment capital and not the misrun ones which are not.

On top of Keynesian policies, there were new healthcare, financial and energy regulations making the future outlook for business uncertain and expensive. Adding to these regulations were a host of new tax increases that squeezed budgets making expense cutting, i.e., downsizing, the only path to improve the bottom line. The actions from the Obama Administration were like someone threw a wet blanket over the economy.

With the Keynesian model in full force and the economy still just barely chugging along, people weren't too optimistic about the future. When workers in mass cling to their jobs as if it's the difference between survival or getting booted off the island, then it's evidence there isn't a jobs' oasis elsewhere. The people who are working will then limit their consumption out of fear of losing their job and paycheck, which means less income generation and low economic growth.

Supply Side Confidence

You could characterize the expression for supply side economics as simply S ▷ D. All this says is supply works to satisfy demand. The sideways pyramid points to demand because of the work required in building a pyramid to reach the pinnacle. If you want a job or to sell a product, it takes preparation and hard work in order to be able to meet demand. Once demand is met, though, income is created and with that, the power to demand products or investments yourself. As a result, other supply works to satisfy the newly created demand. The expression just repeats.

There is no equation where government invests in one side or the other to raise employment. Supply side theory relies on the premise freedom to pursue profit is all that's necessary for economic growth. Give the supply side, which includes business and labor, the freedom to enter the marketplace to earn as much income as possible in equal exchanges, then the economy will grow and so will everyone's standard of living.

The government does play an important role, however, by doing the things markets cannot. The first thing it does is protect private property rights to set the stage for everyone to be empowered to pursue income. The government does many other things like facilitating commerce by building physical infrastructure, investing in scientific research and development, providing primary and secondary education, enacting consumer protection laws, funding space research and exploration, regulating monopolistic powers, protecting the environment, determining proper taxation and so much more.

On a side note, some free market economists believe interest rates should be self-regulating so a Federal Reserve setting the interest rate wouldn't be necessary. There are other things the government currently does or has done that may be better off within a free market framework too such as space exploration, rail transportation, utilities and postal services.

Recessions occur as a result of declining business and consumer confidence. Confidence could be affected by events or bad economic climates such as pandemics, war, terror attacks, oil price hikes, natural disasters, downturns in other economies, or some financial crisis.

The question to ask, how do you improve confidence? Obviously, the first thing is to address whatever caused the panic or economic shock. Some threats can be mitigated with good government policy. For example, the Trump Administration deregulated the energy sector so the country could be on track to become a net exporter of oil in 2020.[40] Being a net exporter has the major economic benefit of our economy not being susceptible to trouble elsewhere affecting the foreign oil supply.

Besides addressing the root cause of a recession, the remedy for a demand shortfall in a recession is allowing markets to reach a new equilibrium, which precludes government spending and easy money. Prices and wages have to be allowed to decline to prevent massive unemployment. Once the new equilibrium between supply and demand is reached, the economy can once again grow.

Sticky wages, which is when employers are reluctant to lower wages, is a real issue. A good idea is for employee agreements and labor contracts to be structured to have a floating salary staying within a specific range.

A floating salary would start with a base salary or wage amount that could decrease in bad economic times and increase in good times. If the economy slumps for whatever reason, the salary would automatically adjust lower. If the economy is booming, then the salary would increase by some percentage.

There should be an automatic trigger instead of leaving it up for people to decide. It could be triggered by a company's own stock price, the S&P 500 Index or some other method yet to be invented. For example, if the S&P increases by 10% in a month, year-over-year, then the salary would increase by an agreed percentage. Conversely, if it declines by 10% YOY, then so would the floating wage decline.

Employee raises, then could be based on the success of either the company or the economy. This would align employee's goals with that of the company, which is to meet customer demand to earn revenue. As the economy grows or inflation increases and employee wages have reached the high end of the range, the base amount can be adjusted to once again align both parties' interests.

By having compensation plans reflect the possibility of lower wages, it should incentivize employees to plan accordingly by budgeting with a lower amount and saving the rest. If their salary declines due to a recession, they could optionally stop their saving plan until their salary once again adjusts higher.

In addition to letting markets work, government policy should be to improve the confidence of both the supply side and the demand side. If one of society's objectives is a strong labor market, then the business climate has to become confident about the future. When businesses believe their investments will result in revenue growth, they'll hire people. A strong labor market is what improves consumer confidence.

Improve the Climate of Supply

According to most media, our economy is consumer driven; nearly 70% of GDP is consumer spending. While this appears true by looking at the GDP, which is the value of all *finished* goods, it's completely untrue when analyzing Gross Output (GO).[41]

The Gross Output measurement is for *all* the economic activity in the production of goods and services. So manufacturers and suppliers not included in GDP are included in GO. When you look at the entire output of our economy, consumers account for only about 33% while business spending is over 60%. This truth places the consumer as the minority on the demand side. Businesses buying from other businesses are nearly two times greater.

The reality is, the supply side meeting both business and consumer demand is what drives our economy. The question to consider, why does the demand side spend? Consumers don't take their income and unload it on whatever is within reach. Instead, they spend because the supply side creates products and services they desire. Business spending too is only for products, services and labor that satisfies their needs.

If we can agree spending occurs because the supply side satisfies market demand, then meeting demand by supply should be something that's encouraged. After all, if supply is successful, demand will spend more. The reason the supply side is good at meeting demand is because they want to earn revenue or income. The motivation to earn income is why they work so hard in producing products people desire.

It's equally true for wage earners. They are motivated to learn new skills and work hard to earn an income. Therefore, we should encourage those in the workforce to meet the needs of the ever changing employment market.

When Keynesians declare increasing consumer demand will increase the supply side, they may believe the 70% number. This could be one reason why the left is so focused on government investing on the demand side. But before there are consumers at retail or B2B customers, all are first suppliers of labor, products or services. This is how everyone earns money so they can then demand. What, you don't say?

If you think about consumer confidence, it's really labor confidence, which is on the supply side. Consumers are only confident when their current and future earnings potential is positive. If it becomes negative due to high unemployment and a recession, it will affect their propensity for consumption. Therefore, labor confidence begets consumer confidence.

In order for labor confidence to improve, there needs to be an improved outlook for business. Tax increases, over regulation and government spending are precisely the opposite of what the economy needs to grow.

I'm not advocating against unemployment compensation or for no safety net, but this should only be done temporarily to benefit those adversely hurt by a recession. We shouldn't spend on the demand side thinking it will lead to job growth. Government spending does very little to improve anyone's confidence that would move the needle on employment. Just ask former President Obama.

Preferably, there needs to be a better business climate developed. This is one where businesses are emboldened to invest their saved capital or will borrow money for the purpose of expanding their operations. The reason businesses invest capital to expand, of course, is to earn more revenue. This is a top line pursuit.

An over regulated and taxed business climate will lead to downsizing and layoffs. Instead of searching for revenues, companies look to squeeze out any profit; a bottom line undertaking.

Business expansion is obviously much better because it involves hiring people. A growing job market, in turn, improves labor confidence. The labor confidence improves with a growing job market because workers become confident about their earning potential.

When wage earners have confidence about their future, they'll consume more. With consumers spending money, it then justifies a business's investment and hiring, which keeps business outlook positive and looking to expand further.

This is the loop of confidence. It starts with business, then labor and finally consumer. Improving the economic climate for business will jumpstart income generation all the way around. Not only do businesses and workers consume more, but all the newly employed become consumers as well. All this new consumption circulates within the economy becoming income, then consumption and then income again.

Removing Interference

To improve business confidence, the government needs to get out of the way with less regulation. It should also lower taxes and consequently spend less, which would free up private capital to invest in productive companies.

This prescription is what leads to growth and more employment. Businesses accordingly would not worry about future government compliance issues. Not being burdened will allow them to focus on growing their businesses instead of worrying about just surviving.

A free market economy will grow without government interference. If the supply side is unconstrained, both businesses and labor will then have the incentive to create the most income as possible. As the climate in the economy becomes freer, economic activity will heat up and expand. Instead of a wet blanket thrown over the economy, having more freedom is like throwing kindling and oak logs on it.

This doesn't mean we should have 100% laissez-faire capitalism, but as much as is possible. Laissez-faire is a French term meaning *let do*. In other words, the government should let the economy do what it does without interference. The government's role in our free market economy should be limited as much as is feasible to only do what free markets can't.

An economic system where there's freedom to earn as much income as possible builds supply side confidence for both business and labor. Supply side confidence then results in consumer confidence. As a result of positive confidence covering all facets, our economy will grow and there'll be enough demand for labor for anyone who'll work to satisfy it.

- FIVE -

Private Property

In free market capitalism, there isn't anyone taking an account of organic wealth creation, although many on the political left would like to. For instance, Bernie Sanders (I-VT) has proposed a *national wealth registry* where all assets would need to be reported to the IRS so the government could track each person's wealth.[1] This would require reporting all assets no matter where they are held globally. The point, as expected, would be to tax it every year with a wealth tax. Bernie has said many times, "I don't think billionaires should exist." The registry would be his way of eliminating them.

In a free country, the wealth belongs to the earner, the investor and the entrepreneur all because of our natural rights, which were derived from our Creator. The right to own private property is paramount to our free market system's success. An individual or group cannot forcibly take your property. Doing so has traditionally been recognized by everyone as theft.

The Framers of the Constitution meant to restrict government's taking of private property without due process of law or without paying fair market value. The Anti-Federalists of the time worried of tyranny and wanted to limit the government's power of directly taxing its people. They were concerned the new government could take private property away. We're going into much more about this subject in the next two chapters.

Private property can be separated into two categories, real and personal. Real property consists of immovable objects: land and buildings. Personal property is an object which is movable and can be either tangible or intangible. Examples of tangible property are cash money, cars, furniture, smartphones, clothes and groceries. Intangible examples are paychecks, bank accounts, investment accounts and intellectual property; such as patents, trademarks and copyrights.

Because of our private property rights in free market capitalism, individuals have an incentive to obtain more property to increase their standard of living. This is why capitalism works. People want a better life for themselves and their children so they bring something of value to a marketplace to obtain the most income possible. It's not just to acquire stuff, but it's possessing the freedom to live the life most fulfilling to them. The freedom to pursue self-defined success is the American Dream.

The *incentive* is crucial. With nearly everyone having a motive to increase income; productivity improves, new products are invented and new innovations take place.

The end result of a competitive marketplace is the standard of living improves for all of us.

There are many ways people can become more valuable or marketable to increase their income. They can get a degree or job training, work harder, have a better attitude, do a good job, etc. There's also the opportunity to do a side hustle or do something entrepreneurial, which may provide even greater financial rewards by leveraging the productivity of others.

Most people have the incentive to gain income and act on it. The issue plaguing our society is too much consumption to try to have a better quality of life today. All this consumption takes away the focus of creating wealth so they may have a better quality of life tomorrow.

The good news is we can have the best of both worlds. We need to learn to live within our means while at the same time create organic wealth out of thin air by saving unconsumed income. With this strategy firmly in place, we can then focus on increasing our income to improve our standard of living for both today and tomorrow.

Original Idea

Organic wealth is not a new idea. In fact, it was the original idea. Before monarchs ruled societies, people were free to acquire property through their labor and to trade for other goods. Even biblically, in Genesis 3, God told the first human, Adam, he and all of humanity would have to work for their livelihood, "by the sweat of your brow." In other words, we would need to exchange labor for our sustenance in an equal transaction. From this we can infer the property we work for belongs to only us and not those who sit idly by while we do all the work.

It's self-evident that property belongs to the person who earned it with their labor. If this isn't true, then someone should ask Alexandria Ocasio-Cortez to share her congressional paycheck with them. My guess is she'll say it doesn't belong to the person asking for it because she's the one who earned it. And besides, she would also point out, that she needs it to pay for the high cost of living in Washington D.C.

Undeniably, the property someone earns belongs to only them and they are free to do whatever they wish with it. They can consume their property, store it somewhere, earn an income from it, dispose of it, donate it to someone else or enter a trade with another person for a different kind of property. This is true whether the earned property is money or a natural resource which is acquired through labor.

To possess the natural resource of clean drinking water in sub-Saharan Africa, for instance, many women and children have to walk many miles daily. Even though the water in the river belongs to any passerby, the water carried back in jugs belongs to only those who make the long laborious trek. Everyone recognizes, without some government authority telling us, another party doesn't possess a right to the retrieved water. If an outsider wants some, they better ask nicely or start walking.

Accumulating Property

As a result of the natural right to obtain private property, it's also our right to accumulate property to increase our standard of living. This is likewise self-evident. A person who accumulates property does so over time by exchanging their labor or talent for it.

Most wealth isn't gained in an ill-gotten way, but in equal transactions by being productive and meeting the needs of a marketplace. In other words, wealth is just saved income, which was received in return for providing something else of equal value.

Even inheritances were first earned by someone else who provided equal value for it. The earner of property then has the natural right to donate their property or to give it away to another person as they please. Crooks, on the other hand, don't provide equal value and should have their ill-gotten gains seized.

Think of what is actually occurring when a redistributionist government takes away someone's wealth to give to others. Wealth is really accumulated income or put differently, the value of someone's accumulated labor. They both mean the same thing because money is just a medium of exchange. So it's really labor or talent that's being confiscated for another group's benefit.

A government that redistributes wealth is essentially taking away someone's labor to give to another who didn't labor. It's as if a person fished all day long only to have his catch confiscated to give away to others who didn't fish. The taking of labor from one person, with no benefit given in exchange, to give away for someone else's benefit is theft and ultimately, slavery.

Wealth may also include interest earned and appreciation. So it's not entirely just accumulated labor. Interest earned is currently taxed and paid by the owner so any portion of wealth from interest earned, is after tax interest. Of course, the original income earned was also taxed before it could be saved. Any appreciation in value would also be taxed as a capital gain once the property is sold. The point being is redistribution of wealth is actually confiscated labor (slavery) and double taxation.

The socialist ideas permeating the Democratic Party have redistribution at their core. Former presidential candidate Andrew Yang (D) proposed a universal basic income of $1,000 per month for everyone, but for nothing in return.

Bernie Sanders tackles it another way by proposing a guaranteed job for everyone. This means the government would create jobs for people wherever bureaucrats see a need. It could be sweeping sidewalks, cleaning parks or laying blacktop. Guaranteeing jobs comes right out of socialism where everyone is an economic stakeholder.

A government job is an unequal transaction that shrinks the wealth pie. The money given away to the sidewalk sweeper isn't found in his dust pile. But rather, is confiscated from those who exchanged something of equal value like when they earned it from their labor or talent.

Ownership Rights

The socialists don't respect ownership rights and therefore, don't respect freedom. Once there's ownership in property, a free society doesn't lose their ownership rights simply because they accumulated more than others, or another group determines there's a better use for it. Taking property belonging to someone else is theft, and it always has been.

If a group of people coerce the government to intervene to take property on their behalf, this is still thievery. Albeit, legal theft. Just because a government legalizes theft doesn't mean it doesn't violate one of God's Ten Commandments against stealing.

Legal theft is one reason why socialism runs contrary to liberty and why it violates God's law. Socialism forces redistribution of wealth, which is confiscation of someone's property (labor) to give to others. The unnatural act of redistribution takes away individual liberty and it violates the self-evident law against theft.

If society's members are truly free, then the right to accumulate property must exist. Wealth redistribution abolishes private property rights and carves away at our natural state of freedom.

The mainstream Democratic Party is embracing radical socialistic ideas having first become popular on the far left. They want to prevent too much wealth accumulation from occurring and to also confiscate existing wealth.

The American people, like never before, have to decide between freebies or freedom. They have to choose because they cannot have both.

If we can maintain our liberty, which necessarily includes earning and accumulating property, it will allow the economic system of capitalism to thrive. For capitalism to be successful, though, it requires a free market.

The Free Market

Exchanging property for something else is also a natural right. It's not against nature for an individual to trade a good they possess for another good another party possesses. If both sides agree, then it's an equal transaction and naturally within their rights.

Not only is the ability to trade within our God-given rights, but the new property acquired in the trade is our property too; it's indirectly the result of our labor. Even if we didn't labor for the new property specifically, we labored for the property that was traded away for it.

The freedom to trade also encompasses employing our labor (or talent) and exchanging it for goods, services or for money another entity owns. Obviously, what we receive in return from our labor is also our property. This means when we go to work every day, the paycheck we receive in return from an employer belongs to only us.

This natural freedom we possess, trading with others, is the free market. Ancient Greek philosophers didn't discover the free market and we didn't need to form a government so we could have a free market. A free market was self-evident!

Though the free market was evident, over time barriers to the free market were constructed by governments thereby diminishing the wealth potential for society. Mercantilism, for example, restricted imports because they believed wealth was zero sum. Mercantilist governments of the 16th to the 18th centuries didn't want gold to exit their country by purchasing goods from another country. They believed to build wealth, the nation's objective should be to accumulate gold with exporting and not by spending it away to make another nation rich.

The philosopher and economist Adam Smith (1723-1790), is credited for his insight trading with other nations actually made a nation wealthier. The wealth of a nation isn't the amount of gold it possesses, but it's the gross domestic product it produces through trade.

The key is for a nation to produce and export what it's good at. When inefficiencies exist, however, making production difficult, then importing from other economies is more beneficial. It's better because the imported goods allows a nation to have access to essential goods that will further commerce such as with raw materials. In addition, imports will improve society's standard of living.

Donald Trump was often characterized by some free trade elites as a mercantilist because he was concerned about trade deficits. There is a cause of concern his critics don't ever acknowledge, however. When products are purchased from other nations, the money circulates within those other economies and not within the United States. Instead of money going from income to consumption to income again within our economy, it just leaves.

The question to ask these informed free traders, with all things being equal, what's better for the U.S. economy, buying a product from another nation or buying from an American-based company? Obviously, buying in the U.S. is better because money circulating within our economy means more jobs.

Someone who is concerned about trade deficits doesn't seek a reduction in imports, apart from wanting to make the companies within the U.S. more competitive but instead, seeks to increase exports. A fair trade philosophy requires demanding access to overseas markets when the trade gap is significant.

As such, a $500 billion dollar trade deficit with China means we've been pumping a half a trillion dollars from our income/consumption cycle to circulate within China creating organic wealth over there instead of here. In a fair trade relationship, China would buy more from U.S. firms, which adds to the volume of our income pool. Ergo, we would have the best of worlds: free trade (aka cheap products) and organic wealth being created within the good ol' USA.

In The *Wealth of Nations*, Adam Smith introduced the idea of *the invisible hand*,[2] which is that the individual self-interested actions in markets actually made a society more prosperous. Smith didn't discover the free market, however; it intuitively always existed just obstructed by government control. His insights have led many to describe him as *the father of modern capitalism.*

Trading with others and obtaining private property is a fundamental human right. Any government that prohibits trading within a free market or confiscates private property to redistribute violates our natural rights and reduces individual liberty.

The prerogative to engage within a free economy is the great equalizer in society and needs protection. The free market doesn't provide equal outcomes, but it does provide the equal opportunity to achieve success and for anyone to improve their family's standard of living.

Pursuit of Happiness

Accessing the free market to earn income by exchanging something of equal value enables people to become self-reliant. As a result of meeting demand, there's no need to rely on a benevolent king or some government provision. The free market bestows independence upon the individual. Not being dependent upon the government is a recognized founding unalienable right otherwise known as the pursuit of happiness.

People in a free market system possess the freedom to bring something of value to a marketplace. Therefore, the only barrier standing in the way of improving one's standard of living is meeting demand. It's not an oppressive government, a lack of resources to redistribute or a thwarting of potential success with an unscalable mountain of red tape.

Self-dependence is better than government dependence because each person then has control of their own destiny. In addition to providing basic needs such as food, clothing and shelter, meeting market demand gives anyone the opportunity to earn more than just enough to survive. This is the greatest promise of a free economy.

The freedom to engage in a competitive marketplace opens the door for everyone to prosper by building organic wealth. The promise is you get out what you put in. Even if what you put in means working a few more hours or taking on an extra side job, a free market allows members of society to prosper.

People can move out of poverty in America because no one was given the poverty imprisonment life sentence. Only within free market capitalism can people, who are willing to work for it, be self-empowered to improve their lives. Socialism promises to give you a lot of things, but it certainly doesn't give you that.

Fundamentally, the right to own and accumulate private property is indispensable to a free market. Without the basic right to private property, there wouldn't be the necessary incentive to compete in a marketplace. With private property protected, a competitive marketplace thrives as people work to create the most income as possible. The end result of having this incentive is the standard of living for all of society continually improves over time.

Property Rights

If an individual was living alone in some land, without a governmental system established, it would be completely natural for this person to acquire property through their labor. No one would doubt this person's claim to their property, which they acquired living alone.

But what would happen when another person, some other family or a whole tribe enters the scene? If the newcomers were also concerned about their own property, establishing property rights would be one of the first orders of business. Land boundaries would need to be established and so too rules governing enforcement of each owner's real property rights.

Personal property in like manner would need rules protecting an owner's rights. A wanderer couldn't trespass on another's land and take livestock as they pleased. Movable property couldn't be fair game; otherwise, chaos and a breakdown of the society would take place. Personal property, therefore, requires protection with well-established ownership rights.

The new members of this society would naturally want to ensure their livestock and other property they brought with them was protected. They wouldn't necessarily trust those who occupy nearby land. It would be in the best interest of all parties to establish real and personal property rights which equally protect each member.

When contemplating setting up a government, members of this free society would naturally only agree to a system protecting each member's property rights. It would go against nature to agree to any other government. For instance, members wouldn't agree to submit to a government that redistributed their property simply because other people had less than they did.

Attempting to convince society otherwise isn't natural. Socialism, therefore, isn't natural either. Within this system productive property belongs to the public and there's a limit on how much one may acquire and accumulate.

There are several rights associated with property, which are the natural rights of a free people. Without a government, all these rights would be established by free people to protect one another's property. Any other system violating these rights runs contrary to natural law.

Acquiring Rights

The right to acquire property is foundational. It's the ability to engage within a free market to earn property such as income. In addition, these acquiring rights extend to our ability to exchange or trade for other types of property. It's only natural for a free people to have the right to obtain property.

One of the great benefits of acquiring property is that it may store value. This allows people to build their wealth over time. For example, real estate can appreciate steadily and can potentially provide rental income.

Other benefits arise from the right to acquire property that satisfies demand. When demand is met, it means the customer's needs are being fulfilled, which improves their standard of living. Meeting market demand also allows the income earner to then demand other products and investments of equal value.

Accumulation Rights

Accumulating property, which was acquired by meeting demand, is basically property exceeding consumption. This right is in danger because there's a political party wanting to enact a wealth tax. This would empower the government to take away a person's private property because they've determined there's a better use for it or because they have decided it's the fair thing to do.

The ability to accumulate property doesn't just mean the right to obtain what you need, but it's the right to obtain as much as you want. Having the right to acquire more than you can consume is imperative for a society to be free. If we couldn't acquire more than a set amount, then the wealth pie would stop expanding or even decline. Limiting accumulation would place our standard of living in jeopardy because it removes the incentive for people to satisfy marketplace demand.

Financial Rights

Possessing the right to obtain and accumulate property results in the natural right to gain whatever financial benefit arises from that property. A free people can earn income from leases and rents, interest from savings, and dividends from investments. They are also entitled to any appreciable gains once the property is sold. For a government leader to say, "You didn't build that"[3] goes against God's intent for us to be free.

Transfer Rights

With the acquirement of property, the owner of the property has the natural right to dispose of it however they choose. The owner can transfer their ownership rights to another person or entity as a gift, or by selling the property for money.

The new owner will then have complete ownership rights over the property. These transfer rights should extend to when a person dies. Their estate should be free to transfer property without a government intervening to take any portion of it.

Enforcement Rights

All the previous rights are powerless unless society protects those rights with clearly defined enforcement rules. One important role of government is to enforce contracts between parties and to resolve disputes.

Property is Freedom

If socialists or pro-redistribution liberals get their way, then they'll determine what is too much property owned or too much property earned. Punishing success or prudence with high income taxes, death taxes or a wealth tax to give away to others violates our natural right to obtain and accumulate private property. Individual liberty is what's at stake.

Many of these progressives in the Democratic Party are not concerned about natural rights, but instead want to give other people's property away by making up new, unnatural rights. Democratic socialists and other liberals desire political power obtained by the votes of one group of people in exchange for free things such as debt forgiveness, paid college, free health care and a basic income. They label these benefits for their quid pro quo as basic human rights.

It's illogical to refer to these freebies as rights, however. How can something be a right that costs money? If it requires another person to pay for it, then you are necessarily forcing one group to work for another group's benefit. Not only is this theft, but like I've already stated, it's ultimately slavery.

The Bill of Rights in the U.S. Constitution was added to protect our actual real rights, otherwise known as our liberty. The Constitution doesn't give us these rights, but prevents government from abridging these natural rights which God intended.

When people say Americans have freedom they are referring to individual rights such as free speech, freedom of religion, the right to assemble, the right to bear arms, having a free press, freedom to petition the government, the right to privacy, personal private property rights and the freedom to pursue happiness, which includes earning an income.

How free would we be without free speech? If only sanctioned speech was accepted, then other ideas would necessarily be criminalized. A government with the power to criminalize speech would become tyrannical and the citizens would become its subjects. Even now, our freedom of speech is threatened by those who are advocating for hate speech laws.

These social justice warriors want to outlaw speech they deem offensive; effectively turning citizens against one another at the workplace, school, church or any public arena. Don't dare use the pronouns her and him, say an unborn child is a person, or assert Jesus is the Way. That might offend a protected person or group.

Political speech is also being silenced or discredited; not by the government, but by social media and big tech companies. No matter your political leanings, we need to push back against them for doing so. When these companies filter out conservative opinions and ideas, they are promoting one world view above another based on their own political biases.

Even though these companies are private enterprises, the same principle applies. The marketplace of ideas perishes and with that freedom dies. It may not be the government becoming tyrannical, but the promotion of just one side, as a result, will shape public opinion and eventually, public policy.

The same question can be asked about private property rights and the ability for someone to earn an income. How free are we without the right to obtain and accumulate private property? If the property someone works for can be taken away, then what incentive is there to be productive and successful? The right to pursue the American dream, as each person defines it, would diminish. Individual freedom is inherently linked to the right to obtain and accumulate property.

Not only is the opportunity for success lost, but if property can be taken away for some virtuous use, as determined by government rulers, then who has all the power in society? It wouldn't be the individual, but the government would have all the power.

A government supplanting its virtues above the individual does so corruptly because it's solely on gaining or maintaining power. When a government possesses the power over the wealth of society, it will become tyrannical by dictating whatever the ruling class desires. Freedom is lost as the right to determine the best use of one's private property is lost.

As we'll see in the next chapter, the right to obtain and accumulate private property was something the Founders sought to protect within the U.S. Constitution. To push back against progressives who continually seek to undermine this ideal through the tax code, a constitutional amendment may be necessary. Let the States determine how many free things they want to give away and let them raise their own revenue to pay for it.

- SIX -

Power Restrained

With the left's ramped up campaign against wealth creation and accumulation, we only have a minority of elected officials, equivocal people in black robes and our Constitution standing in their way. With progressives taking over the White House and Senate in 2021, they've come to outnumber those who believe in limited government. That leaves a courteous GOP, the Supreme Court and the Constitution as our last bulwarks of opposition. Of course, the goal of progressives and socialists will be to institutionalize one-party rule, pack the Court and eventually replace the Constitution. But until then, the left's power to enact redistribution of wealth policies can only go so far.

After the War of American Independence, the very first constitution we had was called the Articles of Confederation (1781).[1] This organizing document created a confederation of the thirteen colonies, which together were called the United States. The national government was extremely weak, though. The Articles made clear that each of the states were to retain, "its sovereignty, freedom, and independence, and every power, jurisdiction, and right, which is not by this Confederation" (art. II). The new United States of America wasn't much unified.

Despite the national government being nearly powerless, it still had three important mandates: "The said States hereby severally enter into a firm league of friendship with each other, for their *common defense, the security of their liberties,* and *their mutual and general welfare*" (art. III; emphasis added).

The national government was weak because the Articles didn't provide a taxing or enforcement authority so it couldn't really do much to fulfill its objectives. The Confederation Congress would just make a requisition to each state to raise revenue, which was proportional to their land value. Then, each state's legislature would impose taxes in the method of their choosing.

The third mandate, *mutual and general welfare,* didn't mean Congress was given carte blanche to spend money however it pleased. It was nonspecific because of unforeseeable needs the country would face. Nevertheless, the word welfare was restrained by the qualifiers, mutual and general. Any spending had to be mutually and generally beneficial to all the States and not specifically benefiting just one.

For example, the Confederation Congress couldn't spend money exclusively to build up Maryland because the other twelve states also paid into the Treasury. It would be absurd to say spending national revenue to construct roads and bridges all over Maryland would be good for all the States and therefore qualifies as *general* welfare. For anybody to use that type of reasoning, it would make a mockery of the Founders' intent.

Qualifying the word welfare with mutual and general was applicable to the States and not to the citizenry. In other words, as far as spending goes, the national government's constituency was the state governments. This is because the revenue was received from each state and not by taxing people or commerce.

The Confederation ended up being ineffective because the national government was unable to fulfill its objectives. To fix its shortcomings, a Constitutional Convention was convened. The first resolution proposed was:

> 1. Resolved that the articles of Confederation ought to be so corrected & enlarged as to accomplish the objects proposed by their institution; namely, "common defense, security of liberty and general welfare."[2]

The Convention turned from being a fix to a complete replacement. The Constitution replaced the Articles of Confederation and it also used the terminology, general welfare, in two areas. The first place is the Preamble which almost uses the exact language as the Articles of Confederation, "common defense, security of liberty and general welfare." It leaves out mutual.

The second place was in the Taxing and Spending Clause. This clause gives Congress the power to tax the citizens to raise revenue and to spend money: "to pay the Debts and provide for the common Defense and general Welfare of the United States" (art. I, sec. 8, cl.1).

Again, welfare is only qualified by general. It's reasonable to conclude the Founders wanted spending to be restrained to only general needs and benefits. They removed mutual because they weren't requisitioning the States any longer since the new Constitution gave Congress taxing authority over the people and commerce.

Therefore, it couldn't be for the mutual benefit like it was previously because the constituency changed. The new Congress was taxing the people, not the States, so it could only be for the general benefit of all the taxpayers. Mutual benefit would be an impossible standard.

General welfare *should* mean any spending of our tax dollars shall generally benefit all taxpayers and not just some. Giving money to a single congressional district, for instance, doesn't benefit all the taxpayers. It's absurd to those taxpayers living on the other side of the country to call it general welfare. In the same vein, giving some people the wealth confiscated from another group is not general welfare to all the taxpayers.

If the Founders indeed desired to restrain Congress's power to spend, it was all for naught. The Supreme Court has ruled that it believes defining *general welfare* should be left to Congress and not to the Court. This deference of the Court's power then empowers Congress to spend revenue as it pleases. Thanks to Court precedence, there are no restraints in what the legislature decides to allocate money for. This is why we run a massive deficit and why our national debt is obscene.

As far as spending goes, Congress has unlimited power to spend tax revenue as it wishes because general welfare no longer has any meaning. Congress can provide a basic income, pay off some college debts, give "free" healthcare to illegals or redistribute wealth as it imagines accelerating our path to socialism.

There is a glimmer of hope, however. It's possible that enough people will reject these socialistic ideas and vote for those who want a limited government at all levels of government. If the numbers are sufficient and to fulfill Donald Trump's edict, "we will never be a socialist nation," amending the Constitution may be what's required. To restrain spending, we need a balanced budget amendment and another amendment prohibiting, or severely limiting, the possibility of redistributing wealth.

Two amendments such as these will slow the leftists down. I propose the Organic Wealth Amendment in the next chapter, *Taking by Tax.* At least something similar to this should be debated by the States.

The Supreme Court has forever ensured Congress would have unchecked power to spend. Even though this is true, their power to tax to raise money is partly restrained—well, at least for now.

The importance of limiting Congress's taxing authority during our founding was to protect existing wealth within the States. Nowadays, many claim a wealth tax is constitutional. For the remainder of this chapter, we'll examine Congress's constitutional power to determine whether wealth is safe from Washington's reach.

Power to Tax

The main issue with the Articles of Confederation was it didn't provide the federal government with an adequate and reliable source of revenue. This became painfully clear during *Shays' Rebellion* in 1786 and 1787.[3] Daniel Shays, whose last name is forever linked, reluctantly and partially led former Revolutionary soldiers, turned farmers, in acts of insurrection.

The armed group closed down courthouses because of the many foreclosures and imprisonment of farmers who couldn't pay their debts or taxes. The farmers used a barter system to trade their agricultural products because paper money was scarce. With no currency, they had no ability to pay what they owed. The farmers' treatment was unjust, but the revolt threatened the fledgling country's attempt at independence.

The national government was incapable of helping Massachusetts gain order because Congress had no budget to pay an army or militia. If the government couldn't help with an internal rebellion, the country would be seen as feeble and would be just inviting an attack from a hostile foreign power such as from Great Britain.

The uprising was the final straw in the minds of many, including George Washington. After leading the Continental Army to victory in the War, Washington retired to his home in Mount Vernon, VA. The former General became greatly concerned about the new government and the welfare of the country. As such, he was persuaded to attend the Convention in Philadelphia and was unanimously elected to preside over the assembly that would eventually write the new U.S. Constitution.

As a result of the Convention and the Constitution's subsequent ratification, the nation was no longer a confederation of friendly states. Instead, the country became a constitutional republic with a much stronger federal government that would no longer rely on the States for revenue. It had the authority to implement taxation and the enforcement power to collect.

The taxing power fell on the legislative branch. Despite the fact Congress was given the authority to tax, its power wasn't unlimited. This is especially of interest in our day with the rise of socialists within the Democratic Party. Congress's power to tax is derived from the Taxing and Spending Clause:

> The Congress shall have Power To lay and collect *Taxes*, *Duties*, *Imposts* and *Excises*, to pay the Debts and provide for the common Defense and general Welfare of the United States; but all Duties, Imposts and Excises shall be uniform throughout the United States; (US Const. art. 1, sec. 8, cl. 1; Emphasis added).

To better understand this clause, we need to define the following terms: taxes, duties, imposts, excises, indirect taxes and direct taxes.

The general term, *taxes*,[4] was understood in the Founding Era to mean any levy where the primary purpose was to raise revenue, but that didn't include a levy with the purpose to restrict commerce like with a tariff.

At first glance, the power to impose taxes seemingly gave Congress the absolute right to pillage society simply by calling something a tax. As we'll soon discover, however, that interpretation is not valid. Before we define the remaining three taxation terms (duties, imposts and excises), we need to break down *taxes* further. There are two different categories of taxes: indirect and direct.

Indirect taxes are impositions from the government falling on entities engaging in taxable commerce, but the tax flows within the product's price to the actual taxpayer, the consumer. Gasoline excise taxes today, for example, are imposed on gas stations, but it's the motorists purchasing the fuel who pay the tax. They just don't pay it directly to the government.

Direct taxation *should be* pretty straightforward. It's any tax imposed directly on the taxpayer. There are no middlemen. The taxpayer pays the tax to the government or its representatives.

The remaining three terms in the Taxing Clause are classified as indirect taxes. A *duty* was a broad term specifying taxes, but not direct taxes. The words duty and tax were interchangeable when describing indirect taxation methods such as excise taxes and import taxes on articles of consumption. A direct tax isn't a duty, even if it seems it would make sense since it's your duty to pay your fair share.

The next power to tax within the Taxing and Spending Clause is *impost*. This word describes either a tax or tariff on imports. It's narrower than tax or duty because it only applies to imports. But what makes this different is imposts can describe either import taxes or import tariffs. A tariff is much higher than a tax and is used to discourage importation of specific goods; whereas, an import tax isn't too high and is used to raise revenue.

The last power to tax on the list is *excises*. This type of taxation was a domestic tax on the consumption of particular goods. It's assessed on manufacturers, vendors or merchants, who then pass along the cost of the tax within the product's price to the consumer.

In summary:

Taxes

- I. Indirect Taxes (aka Duties)
    - A. Imposts: An import tax on articles of consumption. (includes tariffs)
    - B. Excises: A domestic tax on articles of consumption.
- II. Direct Taxes: Levies made directly to the taxpayer.

It's important to understand these words to ascertain the intent of the Founding Fathers. Over time, activist judges misconstrued some of the meanings of these terms. As a consequence, the power to tax by the federal government expanded. With such power it thereby reduced our freedoms and decreased our ability to create wealth.

If we the people desire the Constitution to say something different, there's a mechanism for that, which is a constitutional amendment. Activists on the bench who substitute their desires over the Founders' intent are nothing more than subversives to our constitutional republic.

Most of the revenue raised by the government from the time the Constitution was ratified in 1787 until the passage of the 16th Amendment in 1913 was from indirect taxes. These indirect taxes (duties, imposts and excises) were levies for commodities and articles of consumption and had to be uniform throughout the United States.

Uniformity

Congress was limited in how it could collect taxes in two distinct ways, with uniformity and apportionment. First, Congress had to make certain all indirect taxes were *uniform*, "but all Duties, Imposts and Excises shall be uniform throughout the United States" (art. 1, sec. 8, cl. 1). This simply means indirect taxation would fall equally on every one who was the object of the tax. For example, if there were to be an impost on tea, then all those who imported tea would be subject to the same tax no matter the location of the port of entry.

In our present day, the government may impose tariffs for products imported from certain countries, but not for similar products from others. This doesn't violate the Uniformity Clause because the country-specific tariff will be paid uniformly by all importers. Uniformity protects purchasers within the U.S. not the sellers from without.

The Uniformity Clause had several purposes. It ensured the ruling class paid the same taxes as everyone else, the politically connected couldn't be favored with lower taxes, and the majority of states couldn't vote to tax the minority of states unfairly. Uniformity guaranteed equal tax treatment and fairness for everyone.

Income and wealth were relatively safe with the uniformity requirement for indirect taxation. These taxes were imposed on articles of consumption. So if taxes were too high, causing demand to drop, then tax revenues would decline. This placed a natural check on the government to not overtax. In Federalist Paper 21, Alexander Hamilton makes this point to the State of New York:[5]

> If duties are too high, they lessen the consumption; the collection is eluded; and the product to the treasury is not so great... This forms a complete barrier against any material oppression of the citizens by taxes of this class, and is itself a natural limitation of the power of imposing them.
>
> Impositions of this kind usually fall under the denomination of indirect taxes, and must for a long time constitute the chief part of the revenue

> raised in this country. Those of the direct kind, which principally relate to land and buildings, may admit of a rule of apportionment.

There is something from the previous Hamilton quote you should keep in mind. He makes clear if a consumption tax is too high, tax collection is eluded. The amount to the Treasury declines because consumption taxes on products can be avoided by not purchasing those products. This is important because as we'll see in the next chapter, he later argued before the Supreme Court the carriage tax was a consumption tax even though it couldn't be avoided. The tax was compulsory to existing carriage owners. In today's English, that's an oops.

The Framers envisioned that indirect taxation would be the primary source of revenue for the government. They did, however, believe direct taxation should be an option to raise revenue when required. In a national emergency such as war, the federal government would need to have an additional source of funding and couldn't rely on consumption taxes alone.

What are Direct Taxes?

Indirect taxes were limited through uniformity, but what about direct taxes? Allowing the national government the power of directly taxing the people was vigorously discussed and debated before the Constitution was ratified. It wasn't a simple issue and consumed a considerable amount of the delegates' time. The same was true at the state conventions. So what's a direct tax anyway?

A direct tax is assessed directly to the taxpayer as a head tax, a tax based on their real or personal property, or any tax paid directly to the government. This type of tax cannot be passed on to someone else. Examples are income, property and wealth taxes.

If the ruling elites' hands weren't constrained, direct taxation would allow organic wealth to be confiscated by a corrupt government. And, any government seeking to take wealth is indeed corrupt.

This background is important because the left claims the government has the power of taxing society's wealth. They believe the Founders didn't intend direct taxes would apply to personal property nor did they think it was simply a payment made directly to the government.

When considering what a direct tax is, the most intuitive answer is the correct one even in our present era over two centuries later. A direct tax is any imposition made directly to the taxpayer. James Madison used this same logic as seen in Federalist Paper 40, "The confederation itself authorises (sic) a direct tax to a certain extent on the post-office."[6]

Madison referred to the postage paid under the Confederation as a direct tax even though the money didn't go into the treasury. He was referencing the Articles of Confederation, Article IX, "establishing or regulating post offices... and exacting such postage on the papers passing thro' the same as may be requisite to defray the expences (sic) of the said office."

The postage paid by the public to the governmental post office was referred by the future 4th President as a direct tax. In Madison's mind, direct taxation was any charge paid directly to the government.

Of course, Madison was very familiar with its meaning. Direct taxation was commonly used throughout all thirteen colonies. The Founders grew up knowing about them and paid them. These weren't British taxes, but imposed by colonial governments to pay for local development and services.

A thorough account of historical taxation in America, including the Colonial period, was written by Richard Ely, published in 1888.[7] It's evident the colonies used direct taxation, which were direct payments to the government based on personal wealth or income.

He summarized the utilization of direct taxation within the colonies by writing, "Direct taxes (in the colonies) were laid either in proportion to property held, real and personal, or according to income, or as a uniform charge upon the poll, or head."

There was also a British imposed direct tax. The Founding Fathers were obviously very familiar with it. The tax was the Stamp Act of 1765.[8] This was a direct tax, sometimes referred to as an internal tax, on the colonists where many daily articles such as newspapers, playing cards and legal documents had to have a stamp affixed showing they paid the tax. This was not a head tax, but a direct tax to take wealth away from the colonies.

Benjamin Franklin appeared before the British Parliament in 1766 regarding the Stamp Act, and it's undeniable Ben Franklin knew what direct taxation entailed: [9]

> Q. You say the colonies have always submitted to external taxes, and object to the right of parliament only in laying internal taxes; now can you show that there is any kind of difference between the two taxes to the colony on which they may be laid?
>
> FRANKLIN. I think the difference is very great. An external tax is a duty laid on commodities imported; that duty is added to the first cost, and other charges on the commodity, and when it is offered to sale, makes a part of the price. If the people do not like it at that price, they refuse it; they are not obliged to pay it. But an internal tax is forced from the people without their consent, if not laid by their own representatives. The Stamp Act says, we shall have no commerce, make no exchange of property with each other, neither purchase nor grant, nor recover debts; we shall neither marry nor make our wills, unless we pay such sums, and thus it is intended to extort our money from us, or ruin us by the consequences of refusing to pay for it.
>
> Q. But supposing the internal tax or duty to be laid on the necessities of life imported into your colony, will not that be the same thing in its effects as an internal tax?

> FRANKLIN. I do not know a single article imported into the northern colonies, but what they can either do without or make themselves.

There are many other examples of contemporaries of the Convention who understood the meaning of direct taxation. For instance, state delegate John Williams (NY) believed direct taxation could be applied to any personal property. He said during the New York Convention:

> Under this clause may be imposed a poll-tax, a tax on houses and buildings, on windows and fireplaces, on cattle, and on all kinds of personal property (He then lists indirect taxes too.). Every source of revenue is therefore committed to the hands of the general legislature ... which may affect the personal rights of the citizens of the states, and put their lives in jeopardy.[10]

James Monroe, the future 5th President, obviously knew the meaning of direct taxation. He was speaking at the Virginia Convention on the adoption of the Federal Constitution and stated that he would give the government complete control over commerce, but take one power away, that of direct taxation.[11] He called it "the subversion of liberty."

He asked, "What are the objects of direct taxation? Will the taxes be laid on land? One gentleman has said that the United States would select out a particular object, or objects, and leave the rest to the states... Will the taxes be laid on polls only?... On all property?"

Monroe understood direct taxation could be applied to any object that was personal property. He also believed that revenue should only come through consumption and that any deficiency could be accommodated by loans. Therefore, he thought direct taxation was entirely unnecessary. As it turns out, borrowing is how the U.S. finances emergencies (and everything else).

Future judges would actually contend the Founders defined direct taxation as only capitations or land taxes. The evidence from the historical record and the debates of the time severely contradict that idea.

Capitation Taxes

Capitations are a form of direct taxation imposed on the *head* of an individual based on certain criteria. Direct taxes, in contrast, can be levied on individuals, households, corporations, state and local governments or some other entity.

Capitation taxes were also called poll taxes or head taxes. All three mean the same thing. The root word of capitation, *caput*, is Latin and means "head."[12] Poll is a Middle Dutch word also meaning "head."[13] After the Civil War, many in the South disenfranchised African Americans by taxing people before they could vote. They called it a poll tax, but historically a poll tax had nothing to do with voting.

Capitation taxes were either an unvarying fixed amount owed per individual subject to the tax or a fixed sum that could vary depending on the taxpayer's ability to pay. In *The Wealth of Nations*, Adam Smith observed them to be inconsistent in their implementation because of the assessor's opinion, "Capitation taxes, if it is attempted to proportion them to the fortune or revenue of each contributor, become altogether arbitrary."[14]

The most likely first individual progressive tax systems were capitation taxes that were calculated based on one's rank or class in society. In France, there were twenty-two possible classes someone could belong to.[15] Adam Smith wrote about the progressive capitations of England and France in his book:

> In the capitation which has been levied in France without any interruption since the beginning of the present century, the highest orders of people are rated according to their rank by an invariable tariff; the lower orders of people, according to what is supposed to be their fortune, by an assessment which varies from year to year.[16]

Before capitations, direct taxes were levied on land owners or households no matter who the person was or the number of residents. Capitation taxes were created to tax individuals directly in an effort to collect more revenue. They were widely used in Europe and throughout the Colonies, but they became unpopular in America because they were viewed as oppressive against the poor.

James Madison, all the colonists, Dr. Franklin, Mr. Williams, James Monroe, Adam Smith and I suspect all the delegates at the national and state conventions knew what direct taxation meant. The known exception was Mr. King who asked during the Federal Convention what direct taxation was and no one gave an answer. The likely reason no one responded was because it was a ridiculous question. As a delegate attending the Constitutional Convention, he should have known the answer. It may have been akin to Gary Johnson (L) who asked in the 2016 Presidential race, "what is Aleppo?"

Giving the national government direct taxation power over private individuals was one of the most discussed subjects at the state conventions. Amendments were offered and delegates discussed the issue in great detail by hashing out the pros and cons of such power given to the federal government. Of course they knew what it meant. There was no doubt direct taxation meant government control over the wealth of the States. The taxpayer has no choice but to pay direct taxes unlike articles of consumption, which could be avoided by not purchasing those products.

The minority in Pennsylvania who dissented from the ratification of the U.S. Constitution had their objections printed in newspapers. This allowed their anti-federalist reasoning to become widely used in other states. To say the Founders believed direct taxes were only unvarying capitations or land taxes is dishonest. There's no doubt these dissenters knew the definition of direct taxes:

> The power of direct taxation will further apply to every individual, as congress may tax land, cattle,

> trades, occupations, etc. in any amount, and every object of internal taxation is of that nature, that however oppressive, the people will have but this alternative except to pay the tax, or let their property be taken, for all resistance will be in vain. The standing army and select militia would enforce the collection.[17]

Direct Taxes as a Last Resort

Many delegates from the State Conventions thought direct taxation was too great a power to give the federal legislative branch. They wanted to limit that power and proposed a familiar method. If there were revenue shortfalls, the legislature would ask the States to make up the difference. The States could then choose whatever mode they wanted in raising the revenue within their state. If a state didn't comply, they would be charged interest and only then could the federal government directly tax.

Several of the State Conventions proposed limiting direct taxation with an amendment partly saying, "that Congress do not lay direct taxes, but when moneys arising from the impost and excise are insufficient for the public exigencies; nor then, until Congress shall first have made a requisition upon the states, to assess, levy, and pay their respective proportion of such requisition."[18]

The proposal eventually lost support because requisitioning the States was a significant problem with the Articles of Confederation and was why a Constitutional Convention was called in the first place. It would prove unworkable as many states could unite together and refuse to pay. Then the national government would be faced with shortages like it was under the Confederation. This would be detrimental especially in times of emergencies such as war.

Direct taxes were clearly understood by those who wrote our Constitution. If they wanted to make a distinction between different kinds of direct taxation, they could have easily done so, but they didn't. The various kinds of direct taxation (personal property, land, head, income) weren't differentiated because whatever the method, the objective would be the same. It would be to raise revenue from the wealth, not the consumption, of the country.

Apportionment

Despite those who argue for unchecked government power, Congress was restrained in its taxing power regarding direct taxation. The rule controlling its power is the *Apportionment Clause* (art. 1, sec. 2, cl. 3), which mandates, "direct taxes shall be apportioned among the several States." This means the percentage of tax revenue from one state cannot exceed that state's population percentage. So if Virginia had 19% of the nation's population, then the direct taxes raised from Virginia couldn't exceed 19% of the total from all the States.

Having to conform to Apportionment made direct taxation more difficult and could fall on the population regressively. On the other hand, it protected private property and therefore, ensured our freedom.

There were pros and cons of the system, but future judges misconstrued direct taxation's meaning because of their perceived misgivings. By doing so, it undermined the contract between the government and the people. If the citizens desire to change the Constitution, as already mentioned, then their representatives can do so by amending it. That's the correct and orderly process.

The Origin of Apportionment

At the outset of the Constitutional Convention, the second resolution taken up by the delegates was regarding representation in the legislature. They believed representatives in Congress should be proportional and not uniform in number.

> 2. Resolved, therefore, that the rights of suffrage (voting) in the national legislature ought to be proportioned to the quotas of contribution, or to the number of free inhabitants, as the one or the other rule may seem best in different cases.[19]

The delegates differed on how representation should be proportional, either by wealth or by population numbers. Those who thought it should be proportional to wealth believed the wealthy states would contribute more in taxes and therefore should have more representation.

It became apparent that representation based on population would win because of the fact that the numbers of people were often a good indicator of wealth anyway. The more populated a state, the wealthier it would be.

To persuade those who were concerned about protecting wealth, Mr. Gouverneur Morris (PA) advanced the idea, "that taxation shall be in proportion to representation."[20] After concerns it would lead to requisitions, he then afterward changed it by "restraining the rule to direct taxation." The proviso passed was, "provided always that direct taxation ought to be proportioned to representation." This *bridge* mostly ended the debate about whether representation should be proportional to wealth or population. It would be proportional to population while at the same time protecting the more wealthy states by limiting direct taxation to their number of representatives.

There was some debate regarding counting the slaves in the South for representation. There were delegates who were against slavery and didn't want to encourage states in obtaining more slaves to increase their representation numbers. Others in favor of slavery, believed slaves should be counted just like free inhabitants because they contributed to the wealth as much as anyone. The compromise came to be known as the three-fifths rule.

The delegate wanted to avoid conflict of their including slaves (even as 3/5ths) within representation by linking representation to direct taxation instead of the other way around. The provision previously passed was inverted to "proportioning representation to direct taxation."[21]

> Mr. Wilson observed that less umbrage would, perhaps, be taken against an admission of the slaves into the rule of representation, if it should be so expressed as to make them indirectly only

> an ingredient in the rule, by saying that they should enter into the rule of taxation; and as representation was to be according to taxation.[22]

Two months later in the Convention, some delegates believed the clause to be misplaced in Section 2 and motioned to have it removed. Mr. Morris pointed out that it was the end result of the debate regarding representation, which brought up the issue of wealth and the counting of slaves as part of representation. The motion was defeated, however.

The debate over representation is why there are two clauses in the Constitution that deal with direct taxes and apportionment (Article 1, Sections 2 and 9).

As it turns out, the final draft of the Constitution doesn't link the two at all, but says both need apportionment, "Representatives and direct Taxes shall be apportioned among the several States..." (art. 1, sec. 2, cl. 3).

James Madison didn't note this final change. It may have been the result of Morris himself who thought the bridge of linking the two could be removed since they had already passed their *gulf of conflict.*

Representation could be proportional solely on population because direct taxation would be proportional as well. This would satisfy the wealthy states because they wouldn't have to contribute a disproportionate amount in direct taxes than other states no matter their representation numbers in Congress.

The significance of the issue goes to the mindset of the Founders regarding direct taxes. They understood direct taxation would diminish wealth and sought protecting that wealth with apportionment. The apportionment rule wasn't a mechanism to empower Congress to confiscate as much as they desired just to fritter it away like financial illiterates who just won the lottery.

Not Easily Apportioned

Apportionment is found again, within Article 1, Section 9. It says, "No capitation, or other direct, Tax shall be laid, unless in Proportion to the Census..." (cl. 4)

This clause was originally written without the wording, "or other direct." It just said, "No capitation tax." But during the Constitutional Convention, George Read (DE) moved to insert after "capitation," the words, "or other direct tax." His motion passed and became included in the clause.

The reason for this change was because he was afraid Congress could misconstrue the original clause's meaning. They could take liberty with this rule and use as a pretext that it only says capitation, which are direct taxes levied on each individual subject to the tax. This could open the door for other direct taxes without apportionment. James Madison noted the motion:

> Mr. Read moved to insert after 'capitation,' the words 'or other direct tax.' He was afraid that some liberty might otherwise be taken to saddle

> the states with a readjustment, by this rule, of past requisitions of Congress; and that his amendment, by giving another cast to the meaning, would take away the pretext.[23]

Some states owed money from previous requisitions by the Confederation Congress. Read didn't want those debts to be collected by the new Congress through a scheme of direct taxation. The new rule meant they would have to adhere to apportionment, which would be impossible to implement.

The importance of this is future Courts ruled direct taxes only meant those that were easily apportioned. All others that were not easy, such as income taxes, should be classified as indirect taxes and therefore, not needing apportionment, but just uniformity.

The nature of a tax should have been the criteria. If a tax was pass-through and became part of the price of an item, then indirect. If it were a direct payment to the government, then direct. Instead, they ruled whether easily apportionable or not.

They ridiculously claimed if a tax wasn't easily apportioned, then the Founders didn't intend for the rule of apportionment to apply to it. The inference from Mr. Read's addition of, "or other direct tax," severely contradicts those claims.

The purpose of the change was to make it impossible to collect past debts through direct taxation because the rule of apportionment made it unworkable. Every reasonable person should therefore conclude that the addition of the clause was meant to keep every kind of direct tax that wasn't easily apportioned likewise limited.

If the Framers wanted to restrict just those requisitions from being directly taxed, they would have been specific in their wording. Instead, they used the most broad phrase possible, "or other direct tax."

This was obviously done to ensure direct taxes of every kind would require apportionment. As I previously outlined, the historical record reveals they believed all manner of one's personal wealth was in jeopardy of being taken with direct taxation.

The Founding Fathers understood there were unlimited objects of direct taxation and they made no distinction between easily apportionable or not. It didn't matter to them because their goal was to restrain the national government's power to grab the wealth from the States, but also to still give them limited power in case of emergency.

To say otherwise, implies they were unaware of what direct taxation meant and they didn't believe it could apply to personal property. The record, however, proves these beliefs to be false.

The truth is that wealth tax advocates today oppose the Constitution's mandate of apportionment for direct taxes because it's an obstacle to them. They want to confiscate what others have created to punish success or to finance their socialist goodies. So they'll try the same deceitful arguments believing that today's law makers and justices can't comprehend simple language, are unaware of the world the Founders lived in, and don't know about Mr. Read's insertion.

The delegates passed Mr. Read's motion, most of whom were signatories of the Constitution. There is no better source regarding the Founders' intent than these men.

Incidentally, George Read signed the Constitution twice.[24] The first time was for himself. The second time was on behalf of John Dickinson who was away with a migraine headache. Who knows, perhaps a head tax was its cause.

- SEVEN -

Taking by Tax

As we contemplate the position of a U.S. Supreme Court Justice, we expect the ideal: jurists having the capacity and determination to make honest judgements on whether something is legal or constitutional. They are indeed a member of the Court who's the final arbiter in deciding legality. For certain, we want judges fairly calling balls and strikes. If a pitch is thrown out of the strike zone, it's a ball. No questions, no debates, the count is 1-0. If a judge has to decide whether a law passed by Congress is constitutional, then we want them to do so by looking at the wording of the Constitution. Then, with that knowledge, accurately determine if the pitch has made it into the strike zone.

Suppose a corrupt umpire means a batter to strike out. He'll begin with his desire and proceed to make nonsensical calls. Say the pitcher throws three split-finger fastballs bouncing them before the plate. After the bounce, though, the baseball makes it over the plate. The batter doesn't swing, but he's called out on strikes. The fans would wonder if the umpire was incompetent or if the fix was in. Ridiculous calls cause people to doubt the notion of fairness and equal treatment.

Of course, in baseball there's an official rulebook defining what a strike is, and it probably says it can't bounce first. But in our fictitiousness, let's assume it doesn't specify. It would then be up to the umpire to make a judgement call.

These strike calls by our made-up umpire would be bad enough, but suppose other umpires had to follow this guy's judgement. They too would have to call something a strike that was thrown in the dirt first. Thankfully, for the good of the sport, there's no such thing as stare decisis or precedent umpires try to follow.

The same is not necessarily true in law. Once precedent exists, there's reluctance for justices to question or challenge a previous Court's rationale. The end result, we just get more and more baseballs bounced before the plate. This is not good for the country because the game isn't what it's supposed to be. Instead of the rule book getting updated, the people are left to question the very notion of justice from the Highest Court.

Misconstruing the Constitution

The American people's organic wealth began to be in jeopardy as early as June 1794 when Congress passed the carriage tax bill act.[1] This was not a tax at the point of purchase, but a yearly luxury tax payable by everyone who owned a carriage that carried passengers. Daniel Hylton was one such fellow and he had 125 of them. He refused to pay the tax on the grounds it was an unapportioned direct tax and therefore, unconstitutional. His case made its way to the Supreme Court, which had to decide whether the tax was direct or indirect.

The way Congress saw it, not including Congressman James Madison, this was an indirect tax needing only to pass the uniformity test. Hylton, using common sense, thought it was a direct tax requiring apportionment.

Hylton v. United States was decided in 1796 with four justices of six (two abstained) voted in favor of indirect.[2] This was the nation's first judicial review case and the Court would have been reluctant to question the legitimacy of a legislative act of Congress.

Alexander Hamilton and the Attorney General argued the case on behalf of the government and persuaded the Court the carriage tax was on consumption. The Court agreed it was an excise tax and so ruled it was an indirect tax needing only to pass the uniformity requirement. Hamilton was the former Secretary of the Treasury and believed the federal government should have broad taxing and spending powers.

For some reason, the four justices didn't use the simplest and obvious test on whether a tax was direct; namely, is this tax levied directly to the taxpayer or not? If not, then it's an indirect tax. Since excises, imposts and duties have the nature of indirect taxation, the direct tax question test was all that was needed. Ignoring the meaning of the words, direct and indirect, they instead used convoluted logic and misinterpret, what I believe, was the Founders' intent, save perhaps Hamilton.

Justice Chase

Chase was one of the four who ruled against plaintiff, Hylton, and he more or less captured the Court's reasoning. He believed if there was no clear category for a specific tax, then Congress should be given discretion in determining if a levy needed uniformity or apportionment. Justice Chase rejected the carriage tax was direct because the plaintiff didn't convince him it was. Consequently, deference was given to the legislative branch and he voted against Hylton.

In his written opinion, Justice Chase actually contended a tax could be both, direct and indirect. This admission, in my mind, makes the plaintiff's case to outside observers. He didn't explain how something could be both north and south so we're left to wonder. I see it as a willful misinterpretation of the taxing categories, direct and indirect. Instead of objectively ruling on those categories, the Court ruled on the subjective nature of the tax.

Chase concluded the annual tax was an expense to the owner and therefore an excise. If it's an excise, he reasoned, then it's an indirect tax. The problem with his conclusion is that you can't define excises as simply an expense to the taxpayer. There's more to it than that.

Direct taxes are what's always an expense to the taxpayer, not indirect. Comparatively, state property taxes are an expense to the property owners, but they're not considered excises or indirect.

Indirect taxes, including excise taxes, are not expenses to the taxpayer because they're passed through a third party and become part of the item's price at the point of sale. As far as the consumer is concerned, they're just purchasing an item unaware of the actual tax amount that makes up the item's cost.

The Court was claiming the *yearly* tax was a consumption tax because it becomes part of the cost of the carriage. It would be like saying the yearly property tax that homeowners pay becomes part of the cost of a house. Of course, that is ridiculous.

You can define a consumption tax as impositions on a person's income as they consume it on specific goods and services. Because the carriage owners weren't consuming their income by purchasing anything, the yearly tax wasn't on the owner's consumption of their income, but on their wealth.

Additionally, it's completely optional to purchase a product with a consumption tax attached to it. If the tax is excessive, making the price of the item too high, it may affect the buyer's decision.

The carriage tax was a newly imposed tax which would be payable every year. The owners of these buggies could not foresee the yearly tax at the time of sale because the tax didn't exist at that point. Had they known, it may have influenced their buying decision. Since they couldn't contemplate the true cost of the carriage, there's no way it should have been considered a consumption tax. Hamilton should have known better.

More importantly, the tax was paid directly to the government and not through the merchant selling the carriages. Since it was directly imposed on the taxpayer, it was clearly a direct tax.

Justice Chase also said, "A general power is given to Congress, to lay and collect taxes, of every kind or nature, without any restraint." He then added if a tax cannot be reasonably applied, then it shouldn't be subject to the apportionment rule.

And that's the point, the apportionment rule was meant to put a check on Congress to protect the wealth within the States. Why else would the rule be there? If only easily apportionable was the Founders' intent, then they only needed the Uniformity Clause because it would accomplish almost the exact same thing as Apportionment. For example, taxing everyone the same amount, say $100 per head, passes the uniformity text and it's easily apportionable. The outcome is precisely the same.

Even if he was correct, that Congress only conceived of easily apportionable direct taxes, which there's no evidence of this, only to the contrary, that doesn't change the Constitution. It says what it says. He should have told Congress to go pound sand and if they wanted an expansion of power to amend the Constitution.

The case was lost because the Court misconstrued the meaning of direct taxation; they only conceded easily apportionable. Instead, they viewed the carriage tax as an excise, which is a consumption tax. They failed in the first test of whether it was direct and then failed again in their justification for indirect.

The Court, as I see it, should have found the case in favor of Hylton and classified the carriage tax as direct. It doesn't mean carriages couldn't be taxed, just not so by the Federal Government without apportionment. The object of luxury taxes and most other direct taxes should have been left to the States, which have no prohibition against direct taxation.

Direct Taxation Cases

More than seven decades after the Hylton case, the Supreme Court ruled on additional cases regarding direct taxation. Unfortunately, they called wild pitches thrown in the dirt as strikes following the same precedent as Hylton. The most egregious error, in my opinion, was not correctly interpreting the two taxing categories, direct and indirect.

The Founders didn't intend for Congress or the Courts to determine direct or indirect categorization based on preference or ease of implementation. It should have been pretty straightforward; does the tax get imposed on the taxpayer directly or indirectly? That's it, no confusion or drama necessary.

The second error of the Courts was limiting a direct tax to capitations and land taxes. Clearly, the Constitution says direct taxation should be apportioned, not once, but twice. That should have been enough.

If the Founders intended for some direct taxes to not need apportionment, then there would be some mention of such within the Constitution. Since there isn't, then all direct taxes should adhere to apportionment. It's not like they didn't know the vast numbers of objects that could be subject to a direct tax. Clearly from the debates of the time, partially quoted in the previous chapter, they knew all personal property could be objects of a direct tax.

A brief summary of several of these cases the Court ruled on and a few quotes from its opinion follow.

Pacific Insurance Company v. Soule (1868)[3]

This was regarding a tax on insurance companies' receipts. Justice Swayne delivered the opinion for the court and said, "I am inclined to think, but of this I do not give a judicial opinion, that the direct taxes contemplated by the Constitution are only two, to-wit, a capitation or poll tax simply, without regard to property, profession, or any other circumstance, and a tax on land."

As you can see, Swayne had a very narrow view of direct taxes as a capitation or a land tax. This narrow definition seems to have been taken up by future courts.

Veazie Bank v. Fenno (1869)[4]

This case was about a direct tax on the notes of state banks. They mustn't have known about Mr. Read's inclusion of "or other direct tax." The Court's opinion was direct taxes meant only capitations, taxes on land, and taxes on all personal property by a general valuation.

The Supreme Court stated, "It follows necessarily that the power to tax without apportionment extends to all other objects.... The tax under consideration is a tax on bank circulation, and may very well be classed under the head of duties. Certainly it is not, in the sense of the Constitution, a direct tax."

Scholey v. Rew (1874)[5]

This was regarding an inheritance tax on real estate, which the court saw as income and therefore not a direct tax. This Court didn't believe direct taxes had a settled definition, but somehow believed an income tax wasn't a direct tax:

> Whether direct taxes in the sense of the Constitution comprehend any other tax than a capitation tax and a tax on land is a question not absolutely decided, nor is it necessary to determine it in the present case, as it is expressly decided that the term does not include the tax on income.

Taxing Income

Taxing some articles of consumption was one thing, but being able to tax income before consumption or savings occurs is quite another. All choice then is removed. The income tax must have been the Holy Grail to the progressives of that time who wanted a large national government. But, the U.S. Government back then wasn't Marxist or socialist and wasn't about to take more than was necessary. A catastrophe would be needed and a severe revenue shortfall to justify the income tax.

The country had such a catastrophe when the States went to war with one another. The Revenue Act of 1861 was the nation's first income tax and was signed into law by Abraham Lincoln (R). It was enacted to raise revenue to cover the costs from the Civil War. The income tax rates were increased by the Revenue Act of 1864, amended in 1865. When the additional revenue was no longer needed, the income tax was abandoned in 1872.

The 1864/65 income tax came before the Supreme Court in *Springer v. United States (1880)* to decide on whether it was a direct tax requiring apportionment.[6] The Court concluded, "direct taxes, within the meaning of the Constitution, are only capitation taxes, as expressed in that instrument, and taxes on real estate; and that the tax of which the plaintiff in error complains is within the category of an excise or duty."

So just like that, a tax imposed directly on individuals in proportion to their yearly income was an excise or duty and not a direct tax. They narrowly defined direct taxes, accepting the redefinition of an indirect tax by previous courts all by using precedent. Unfortunately, they followed previous umpires' judgements and disregarded the plain meanings of the direct and indirect taxing categories. The pitcher was allowed to strike out the side.

Character Matters

The argument that an income tax should be defined as an excise or duty falls short. Indirect taxes have two distinct characteristics:

1. They are optional. Someone could avoid paying the tax by not entering those transactions subject to the tax. Entering such transactions is considered a privilege.
2. The cost of the tax falls on an entity, but passes through an article's price to the consumer.

The income tax doesn't share those elements. First, the tax is directly imposed on the taxpayer and cannot be passed on to another party. Second, it's impossible to avoid the tax because as free people, we're not dependent upon the government and must earn an income to sustain our lives. Therefore, they are not privileged transactions but necessary. Additionally, earning an income is one of our inalienable rights, the pursuit of happiness.

We don't have the right to a job, but rather, we possess the right to meet demand within a free market to earn income. Possessing this right, given to us from our Creator, means it isn't a privilege or special advantage bestowed upon us by our government overlords. Therefore, since earning an income isn't a privilege, it shouldn't be viewed as an indirect tax of any kind.

Many who claim the income tax is an excise mistakenly imply excise is somehow connected to the word exercise, which is a privileged action. These two words have no shared meaning, however. The word, excise, is from 15th century Middle Dutch, which meant, "tax on goods."[7]

Since the income tax doesn't share the characteristics of an indirect tax, the next question is, does it share that of a direct tax? I believe the income tax is characteristically the same as that of a capitation or head tax.

The public hated capitations because they were regressive and unfair to the poor. The French and English tried to remedy this by creating many different classes or ranks of people and taxing them accordingly. In the 18th century, they were attempting to impose head taxes based on people's ability to pay.

The United States eventually developed an economic system based on a common currency and created the capability to tax individuals based on their ability to pay. The U.S. income tax is thus an advanced version of the head tax. Instead of a fixed amount imposed on everyone or on those of a particular class, it's directly imposed on each head perfectly based on their earned income.

Pollock v. Farmers' Loan & Trust Co. (1895, 158 U.S. 601)[8]

Fifteen years after Springer, a landmark case was decided profoundly widening the Court's definition of direct taxation. More about the reason Pollock was a landmark decision in the next section, *The Wealth Tax.*

The Pollock case was a split decision (5-4) with the majority ruling in favor of Charles Pollock, the plaintiff. Mr. Pollock owned ten shares of stock in Farmers' Loan & Trust. To comply with the Wilson-Gorman Tariff Act of 1894, which was a flat tax of 2% on incomes over $4,000, Farmers' Loan notified him they were complying with the Act. Charles Pollock sued to prevent Farmers from doing so.

Chief Justice Fuller delivered the majority opinion. The scope they considered was whether the tax on real estate income or from personal property was a direct tax needing apportionment or not. The Court did not consider employment income because, as Fuller noted, "taxation on business, privileges, or employments has assumed the guise of an excise tax and been sustained as such."

The Court concluded taxes on real estate and income from real estate were both direct taxes. They also found taxes on personal property and income from personal property were both direct taxes. Because of these two conclusions, the tax act of 1894 was deemed unconstitutional and void.

The income tax act was void because it was written to include income from real estate and income derived from personal property such as stock dividends and bond yields. Even though this kind of income was ruled direct, general income from earnings was still considered indirect. Congress could have written a new income tax act but chose not to.

16th Amendment

Though the Court still considered taxing income as an excise, unless derived from real estate or personal property, the country was without an income tax. The revenues to the Treasury were mostly from consumption taxes. Progressives began turning public opinion against consumption taxation methods calling them regressive and also demanding the rich pay their fair share. The left hasn't changed their playbook since then; they've used class envy as a tactic throughout the past century.

To answer why Congress didn't just rewrite a tax bill excluding income from real estate and personal property was because this type of income was mostly earned by the wealthy. The majority of Americans weren't heavily invested in the stock market like today with 401(k)s and other retirement accounts. The progressives' goal in reality wasn't to help the poor, but to take organic wealth away from the American people who, in their opinion, accumulated excessive amounts.

The 16th Amendment easily passed through Congress in 1909 and was finally ratified by the States in 1913. This put an end to the arguments on whether income was direct or indirect. Organic wealth was in serious jeopardy from this point forward because if you can't keep what you earn, then obviously it's more difficult to save much of what's left over.

The one good thing about its passage was they did it the right way. The elitists weren't happy with the Pollock decision by the Court so they garnered public opinion throughout the country that a constitutional amendment was necessary. Sure they gained public support by saying all goods would be tax free and only the rich would pay income taxes. This was true at first, but it didn't take long for the income tax to expand to what it is now. Here is the 16th Amendment:

The Congress shall have power to lay and collect taxes on incomes, from whatever source derived, without apportionment among the several states, and without regard to any census or enumeration.

The Wealth Tax

If you search for Pollock online, you'll find many websites summarizing the case and then noting the Pollock decision was nullified by the 16th Amendment. It's true, after the Sixteenth's adoption, all sources of income could be taxed without apportionment. But it's untrue Pollock was negated. In fact, the Pollock decision remains a landmark case and a defense against those who would confiscate organic wealth through taxation.

The reason the Pollock case has such importance is that the Court expanded the objects of direct taxation requiring apportionment. The Court not only concluded certain sources of incomes were direct, which was superseded by the 16th, but it concluded taxes on real estate and personal property were also direct. The new object requiring apportionment was that of personal property. The Court summarized their conclusions as follows.[9] Take special note of the second conclusion:

> Our conclusions may, therefore, be summed up as follows:
>
> First. We adhere to the opinion already announced, that, taxes on real estate being indisputably direct taxes, taxes on the rents or income of real estate are equally direct taxes.
>
> Second. We are of opinion that taxes on personal property, or on the income of personal property, are likewise direct taxes.
>
> Third. The tax imposed by sections twenty-seven to thirty-seven, inclusive, of the act of 1894, so far as it falls on the income of real estate and of personal property, being a direct tax within the meaning of the Constitution, and therefore unconstitutional and void because not apportioned according to representation, all those sections, constituting one entire scheme of taxation, are necessarily invalid.

Personal property, not land or buildings, are individually owned assets with value. Examples would include: cash and cash equivalents, shares of stock, bonds and other debt, art, futures contracts and other financial derivatives, vintage wine, yachts, collectible cars, rare coins, antiques, domains, NFTs, patents and cryptocurrencies.

Real estate and personal property would be the objects of any leftist's wealth tax. So, attempts by socialists to tax personal property or real estate, according to the now established precedent set by Pollock, would be of the direct kind requiring apportionment. This is a serious wound to the redistributionists such as Bernie Sanders, but as we'll see, not necessarily a mortal one.

As a result of concluding personal property taxes were direct, several other cases made their way to the Highest Court. They challenged taxes on the basis they were impositions on objects personally owned. Some of these cases included taxes on business exchange sales,[10] sales of stock certificates,[11] estate taxes,[12] corporate taxes,[13] and a graduated gift tax.[14]

The High Court found in all cases they were indirect excises because the taxes weren't on the property itself, but on "incidents of ownership." In the gift tax case, for instance, the Court ruled the gift tax wasn't a direct tax on the property owned, but on the power to give the property to another.

Basically, the Court said the tax was on the activity of transferring property to someone else and therefore taxable to the giver as an excise, which follows uniformity. Alternatively, if an owner disposes of the property in the trash or sets it on fire, this activity would not be taxable. You just can't give it away without paying a gift tax.

By ruling these taxes weren't on the property and therefore, didn't violate Pollock, the Court further established

Pollock. Because these cases didn't overturn the Court's ruling in Pollock, but focused on the activity and powers of ownership, it further established the now long standing precedent that personal property taxes or a wealth tax that's unapportioned would be unconstitutional.

I'm sure at the time these cases were decided, progressives and big government advocates celebrated and cheered not realizing Pollock was being cemented with regard to personal property taxes. Their ideological offspring are now stuck facing Pollock as if it were a big beautiful wall protecting its citizens.

Indirect Redefinition

Even with Pollock, organic wealth is still in jeopardy. The Supreme Court long ago redefined the meaning of indirect taxation. Indirect taxes should have been defined as third party impositions passed along within a product's price to the consumer.

Instead, the Court changed indirect taxes to allow for impositions made on privileges or activities. This is not only absurd, but quite dangerous. With this definition, any tax could be called indirect. Take, for example, the income tax. It's a direct tax in reality, but was misconstrued as an excise or duty, which are both indirect.

They were able to pull this trick off by saying the tax isn't imposed on the taxpayer, but on the privilege of earning an income. This is nothing less than a redefinition of indirect taxation by our almighty rulers in black robes. It didn't matter to them the tax is imposed directly to the taxpayer who cannot pass along the cost to anyone.

Now let's look at a capitation tax. This is a tax imposed directly on the individual and without debate is constitutionally a direct tax. Using the Courts' logic, however, Congress could impose such a tax using uniformity and not apportionment. All they would have to do is simply declare they're not directly taxing individuals but instead, taxing the privilege of breathing air or for possessing a head or some such nonsense. Merely by applying the Court's rationale, this would no longer be a direct tax; it would be indirect.

Think of the danger of an Elizabeth Warren, Bernie Sanders, Kamala Harris, AOC, or the majority of the Democratic Party, who are undercover socialists, willing to decree a wealth tax. Could they do so using a similar rationale? Well, first let's briefly look at a couple of their other options of taxing wealth.

Options for Wealth Taxation

Any direct tax on wealth passed by Congress would certainly come before the Supreme Court. The wealth tax's legal proponents would need a compelling argument for Pollock to be completely overturned and become just a footnote. This seems unlikely given the Court's current conservative leaning and the long standing precedent of Pollock, though, I don't know what their argument would be. Of course, they could always try to stack the Court with a bunch of activist judges.

Another option would be to gin up public support to amend the Constitution. No doubt they would use class envy tactics, which may work within blue states, but would be very difficult given there are many more red ones. To amend the Constitution the traditional way, they would need to convince 2/3 of both houses of Congress and 3/4 of the States. That's not likely to happen.

Overturning the Pollock ruling or amending the Constitution wouldn't even be necessary, however. All they would have to do is impose a wealth tax on some privilege or activity and not directly on any asset. Then the Court, using their bouncy baseball precedent, would have to rule it's an indirect tax and only needing uniformity. Then, presto, an ultra-billionaire tax that will undoubtedly expand to impact everyone who creates organic wealth just like how the income tax expanded.

What could the socialists tax instead of wealthy heads? Anything really, they could tax the privilege of utilizing investment accounts, bank accounts, trusts, financial advisors, land management companies and so on. They'll figure it out, don't you worry about that. They just have to find a justification to adhere to the Court's long standing redefinition of an indirect tax.

Their wealth tax bill wouldn't be elaborate initially, given its likely challenge. They would begin by narrowly imposing a wealth tax on just one privilege like using investment accounts. The tax would not be imposed on an individual's net worth or assets, but on the privilege of using an investment account.

The IRS would determine the tax owed based on the value of a person's investments just like how income taxes are calculated. The income tax is imposed on the privilege of earning an income and the tax amount is based on how much the taxpayer earns.

When the Supreme Court gives them the okay, Congress can impose all types of wealth taxes using only uniformity. They'll just have to adhere to the Court's redefinition of indirect taxation.

Since progressives will spend $trillions on the environment, health care and other free stuff, it's not difficult to imagine the wealth tax affecting the retirement accounts of the middle class. Given that, the public may not be supportive initially, but this could always change in the future. For this reason, a constitutional amendment is needed so we indeed never become a socialist nation.

Organic Wealth Amendment

Before the Anti-Federalists in Massachusetts would vote to ratify the new U.S. Constitution, they insisted individual liberty protections be first incorporated into the document. An agreement was eventually reached known as the *Massachusetts Compromise*, which would occur after the Constitution's ratification. Amendments for a bill of rights could be proposed and they would have the support of the Federalists.

About a year after the Constitution was finally ratified, Congressman James Madison introduced his twenty amendments in the House of Representatives to create the Bill of Rights.[15] The House passed seventeen with many changes. Those were then whittled down to twelve by the Senate, which the House passed, and they were then given to the States. Two of the amendments didn't have enough support, leaving the final ten amendments, which were ratified by the States in 1791.

The 5th Amendment of the Bill of Rights contains the *Takings Clause*, which states, "nor shall private property be taken for public use, without just compensation" (cl. 5). It's called Takings because it prohibits the Government from taking private property for public use, such as eminent domain, without compensating the owner.

It would seem if the government took property for redistribution, it would require compensating the owner. But unfortunately, this clause doesn't protect America's personal property from being taken by the government through a wealth tax.

This clause doesn't prevent taking by tax because according to the Courts, the Takings Clause refers to the government singling out certain persons and their property. They consider a tax legitimate if it's imposed on everyone equally who would be subject to the tax.

They have also determined the Constitution cannot be contradictory where one section says one thing and another portion says something contradicting it. Each section and clause, therefore, has an application. As such, the Taking Clause cannot contradict the Taxing Clause.

One of Madison's amendments that didn't make it was an addition to the Constitution's Preamble. Madison had thought to interweave the amendments throughout the document, but his colleagues in the House thought that would give the appearance of rewriting the Constitution. A new paragraph at the top of the document, as a result, wasn't supported. In addition, many wanted his existing preamble, which famously begins with, "We the People" to be the first words of the Constitution.

The wording of the unsupported amendment was, "That Government is instituted and ought to be exercised for the benefit of the people; which consists in the enjoyment of life and liberty, with the *right of acquiring and using property*, and generally of pursuing and obtaining happiness and safety (emphasis added)."[16]

Would this amendment have been sufficient to protect against a wealth tax? The clause, "the right of acquiring and using property," is pretty powerful, but it wouldn't have been enough. The reason being, the Constitution also gives Congress the right to tax directly and indirectly. Since the Constitution cannot contradict itself, the Courts would have determined a way for both to be true, which, without a doubt, would have favored the taxing power over protecting property.

New Amendment to Protect Organic Wealth

With that in mind, any new amendment would need to fit squarely within the document without creating contradictions. A conflict would give the Supreme Court the ability to narrowly define the new amendment. In addition, a new amendment should prevent loopholes.

To protect our wealth, an amendment could be written straightforwardly such as; taxes on personal property by the government are forbidden. Though it says what we would want, this would certainly be challenged because the Constitution gives Congress direct taxing authority and with the 16th's adoption, the power to tax income without apportionment. A conflict would exist.

The Court would then have to figure out a way to define the new amendment so it squares with the rest of the document. Who knows how they would solve the contradictions, but the last thing the writers of this amendment would want is for the Courts to get their hands on it.

I believe the best way to write a new amendment would be to define direct taxation, which would imply an indirect definition. This wouldn't prevent a wealth tax, but just define it as a direct tax requiring apportionment. By writing the amendment in this fashion, it would fit nicely within the Constitution without creating contradictions. There would need to be an exception for the power to tax income and gains. Also, an inclusion for gift and estate transfers. I would suggest this wording for debate:

All taxes are direct requiring apportionment that are paid directly to the federal government by the taxpayer and were not passed through from another entity; including gift, estate, donee and inheritance taxes; excluding taxation on all sources of income and capital gains.

You may have noticed the wording has *paid* by the taxpayer rather than *imposed* by the government. If it was stated as taxes imposed directly to the taxpayer by the federal government, it would open the door for a court to conclude a wealth tax isn't imposed directly on the taxpayer but rather, on some privilege. By emphasizing paid removes the opportunity for judicial activism.

Indirect taxation has an implied definition. By clearly defining direct taxation leaves everything else in the category of indirect. The words, "and were not passed through from another entity," will exclude actual indirect taxes from being classified as direct.

The left wants to confiscate at every opportunity, especially when someone dies with a valuable estate. This confiscation would apply to people who transfer property to their family as gifts. This is viewed by the takers as circumventing future estate taxes.

Many progressives believe people who accumulate property don't have the natural right to dispose of it as they please. They believe the government should step in like a thief and take away what was accumulated even though it's after tax wealth. This is clearly double taxation by an oppressive government to the determinant of our rights.

The clause, "including gift, estate, donee and inheritance taxes," would make certain all gifts and estate transfers are direct taxes requiring apportionment, and not indirect with only uniformity. This would ensure that the giver and the receiver are both protected from taxation.

Lastly, "excluding taxation on all sources of income and capital gains," would not disrupt our current system of taxation or contradict the 16th Amendment. If Congress wanted, it could always change how revenue is raised such as changing to a sales or consumption tax.

Those who believe all income taxes should be excluded may have good arguments, but it will be very difficult to pass an amendment going from a progressive tax system to one that's viewed as regressive.

One final point, the basis in property currently gets *stepped up* when a transfer takes place. This is possible because of traditional estate and gift taxation. By removing estate and gift taxes, however, leaves assets with unrealized capital gains. The IRS could change the rules for high valued assets so the original basis is transferred along with the property. Changing the rules on basis would allow capital gain taxation when assets are eventually sold at a future time.

Red Alert for State Elections

It's not easy to amend the Constitution, but the Republicans have an advantage over Democrats. There are many more red states than blue. Article V of the Constitution has a provision for the States to call a *Convention of States* to amend the Constitution. The traditional way requires 2/3 support from both the Senate and the House chambers. But with the convening of a Convention of the States, the consent of Congress isn't required. Here is a summary of how it would work:

1) 34 state legislatures call for a convention. Governor support isn't required.
2) All 50 states send delegates to propose amendments. Only one vote per state.
3) Amendments take 26 yes votes to be sent to the States for ratification.
4) 38 states are then needed to ratify an amendment.

This is why elections for state legislatures are so important. Always vote in these elections to elect the party that will stand for our liberty. Visit the Convention of States website, conventionofstates.com to learn more about the movement to have a convention of states.

- EIGHT -

Democratic Socialism

The democratic socialist movement is becoming more popular every day as proponents dangle free college tuition, healthcare, basic housing, universal income and a guaranteed federal job in front of everyone. These socialists label their Marxist crusade *democratic* to make a point of distinction between historical socialist movements and this supposedly new kind. They call it democratic because they envision public control over all institutions instead of a centralized authority like with a dictatorship.

According to the Democratic Socialists of America website, they believe "that the workers and consumers who are affected by economic institutions should own and control them."[1] What they're advocating for are businesses that are no longer owned by shareholders or individuals, but are owned and controlled by the workers and other stakeholders. They want to change our current system of private ownership of businesses to these worker controlled cooperatives, which would become publicly owned instead. Some believers say the exceptions are major industries like oil and gas that would be owned and controlled by the federal government.

But whether it's a centralized government or this new democratic controlled variety, it's still socialism at its core. There is no other point of distinction between the two beyond democratization.

Historic socialism and democratic socialism are anti-capitalist, anti-free markets, anti-competition, anti-property rights and anti-wealth. In other words, they are anti-freedom. In democratic socialism, like the regular socialism, wealth becomes finite or zero sum. As a result, the pie continually gets smaller.

The most famous democratic socialists on the left are Bernie Sanders (I-VT) and Alexandria Ocasio-Cortez (D-NY). They unabashedly admit as much and don't need Republicans to label them socialist because they label themselves so. Not concealing what they really believe is becoming more prevalent for those on the political left.

It's why the majority of Democrats now support radical policies. They have to take such positions to placate to their progressive base. Some, on the other hand, like Sanders and AOC are from that radical base and are truly working to implement those ideas.

These days, in order to obtain political support from progressives; candidates need to be for open borders, Medicare for all, the Green New Deal, reparations, and a universal basic income plan of one kind or another. Their policies will require wealth confiscation from the producers because it's the only way to pay for it all beyond debt.

This chapter is about aspects of democratic socialism you didn't learn while you were dreaming at university.

Democracy

The woke left has graffitied and torn down statutes of Confederate soldiers in public places all across the country. They are petitioning for the removal of memorials of our Founding Fathers who owned slaves such as Thomas Jefferson and George Washington. Though, Washington freed his slaves after his presidency.

Those with social justice running in their veins want paintings removed they find offensive and are boycotting companies they accuse of being against LGBT people. They are leading the effort to rename streets, schools and are pressuring the U.S. Army because of eight of its bases which are named after Confederate generals.

Five hundred years after Christopher Columbus discovered the New World, the morally superior in this century have found him to be objectionable. They want Columbus Day scrubbed and replaced by Indigenous People's Day because of all the horror following Colombo.

Then there's the ongoing effort to induce professional and collegiate sports teams to rename their Native American team names. Even if the teams and fans celebrate Native Americans, it's still unacceptable by those with torches lit with the dim light of self-righteousness. The names must be burned at the stake.

They've succeeded with football's Washington ~~Redskins~~ and with baseball's Cleveland Indians, which are now the Guardians. The Indian's smiling Chief Wahoo logo had already been driven out leaving a tolerable letter C.

Notwithstanding the left's drive to erase our historical past, confront anything aggrieving a marginalized group, and to cast down all they find deplorable; there are limits even for them. Everything ought to be destroyed, renamed and forgotten with one conspicuous exception—the very name of the Democratic Party.

To those who aren't familiar, the Democrats have a terrible history of discrimination and hatred. They are the party of slavery, the Ku Klux Klan, lynching, Jim Crow laws and segregation. They are also responsible for all kinds of disenfranchisement against Black Americans, Native Americans and women in general.

The propagandists on the left falsely say the two parties suddenly switched in the 1960s. They say this as a way to absolve their party's wrongdoing while projecting their blame to the Republicans. Don't be deceived, however. There's no truth in their disinformation campaign. The GOP has always valued every life, both born and unborn, and did not pick up the racism cause Democrats finally left behind for the sole purpose of surviving politically.

Regardless of their revisionism, they still bare the brand of incredible hatred. Since the party has become woke, why isn't there a movement to change the Democratic Party's name? It seems like there should be a mob gathering everyday outside DNC's headquarters demanding a name change given the party's racism and sexism of times past. So, why wouldn't the PC woke people insist the party abandoned such a remembrance?

I could suggest some new names that would fit nicely. How about the Progressive Party, the Democratic Socialist Party, the Liberal Party or the Socialist Workers Party of America? They could merge with the Green Party too. Then we could talk about green vs. red states.

There's no movement to change the name because it's presumed to stand for *democracy*, which is an essential component of democratic socialism. Dictators have learned they can maintain power with some legitimacy as long as they have elections. To win they cheat, of course, but they also promise to give the people what they want, which is free stuff and to be taken care of.

Democrats too desire political power—not to give away to a dictator, but to have their ideas rule over people. What is the destination they want us to progress toward? It's not to keep the status quo of capitalism, free markets, property rights, organic wealth, individual responsibility, and other glorious things they want to upend.

Some Democrats hold this answer closely to their chest not wanting to turn away uninformed moderate voters, while others proclaim it openly. Their desired destination is none other than democratic socialism. The progressive base, though, has been getting impatient with the apathetic small step taking.

Taking incremental steps isn't considered progress anymore because a big orange man can come along and push everything back two steps. So they're demanding the Democrats fight at all costs for their utopian dreams.

To get to their desired destination, they need to win elections the old fashion way. Doing so way will require convincing the public that socialism rocks. Another option is to devise a plan to cheat like other socialist leaders do.

They could always have a revolution, but as of now, their only muscle is Antifa, Black Lives Matter, big tech companies, and some deep state government types. These groups have shown the propensity to burn down city streets, overthrow police stations, take over city blocks and sabotage their political opponents. But overthrowing the entire country? They're not quite there yet.

Without the possibility for a revolution, it leaves elections as their only real option. When Donald Trump surprised them by winning in 2016, they reacted by accusing him of treason, said he was illegitimate and denied him due process while attempting to bring him down.

They were victorious with their puppet in the 2020 election due to the black swan event aka, COVID-19. Winning elections, legally so or not, gives them the power to fully dismantle our system, piece by piece. The only surviving relic of the American experiment that will remain will be a dictator's favorite tool, *democracy.* The transformation must have the pretense of legitimacy after all.

Electoral College

The only thing that prevented Hillary Clinton from becoming president was the Electoral College. Hillary always points out she won the popular vote as if that were more important than winning electoral votes. For those on the left, though, winning the popular vote is everything. It's their very identity as Democrats.

The United States wasn't formed as a democracy; it was created as a constitutional republic. A constitutional republic is a form of government where power is in the hands of the people and those who they elect to be their representatives. The representatives then create laws aligned with a constitution. A key benefit is a representative government protects minority rights because elected officials are more likely to represent all their constituents and not just the majority.

Pure democracy, on the other hand, is a system where laws are created by a vote of the public. If there are a set of by-laws, those too can bend by the will of the people. One of the flaws is this system doesn't protect minority interests because the majority vote will always prevail.

In Federalist 10, James Madison warned of democracies. He wrote, "Democracies have ever been spectacles of turbulence and contention; have ever been found incompatible with personal security, or the rights of property; and have in general been as short in their lives, as they have been violent in their deaths."

The Electoral College was created with the same principle in mind as a republic, to protect the rights of the minority. In presidential elections, smaller states have a say along with the larger more populous ones. There is democracy within each state where the people vote for a president and the winner essentially receives the state's electoral votes. Maine and Nebraska are the exceptions where electoral votes can be split up.

If the Electoral College was discarded, it would mean presidential elections would be determined by a popular vote. The problem is the smaller states and even mid-size states could be disenfranchised by the larger ones. The battlefield for the presidency would then be fought mainly in our largest states, ignoring the concerns and values from the smaller.

The arena of ideas, as a result, would mostly embody the interests from greatly populated urban areas instead of from those across the entire nation. This happens to be exactly what the Democrats want. The reason is obvious, big cities are concentrated with their base of progressive voters while white supremacists live everywhere else.

What does the progressive base want? Well, they want free stuff, of course. Obama gave away phones and EBT debit cards and he was hailed a hero. Today, the left want much more: free healthcare, free college, debt forgiveness, reparations, equity, a guaranteed job and $1,000 a month or more in walking around money.

If the Democrats could rid themselves of the Electoral College, they could then forever be in power and begin implementing their socialistic agenda. By winning the popular vote, they would have a mandate and could say, "It's what the people want." Any remaining conservatives in Congress would get blown over like a house of cards.

Immigration

You don't have to wonder why the Democrats have gone crazy over illegal immigration. The party has shifted from covertly to overtly embracing open borders and legalization status for all, which they refer to as comprehensive immigration reform.

When immigrants legally take root, who also expect government giveaways, democracy will work well for Democrats. They'll then be able to easily win the Presidency, both houses of Congress and many state offices as well. The archaic Electoral College will be but a memory of an old fashioned, out-of-date system, but will eventually be burned to the ground nonetheless.

The importance of democracy within democratic socialism goes beyond just elections for political offices. It's how the left packages socialism to sell it as something noble and good. In democratic socialism just about everything is democratized including corporations, government services and publicly owned resources. The stakeholders vote on how they are managed, how its resources are allocated and so on. Who wouldn't want that, a pay raise by vote?

Social Control

An important feature of democratic socialism is the idea of social control, which really just pretties up the packaging of traditional socialism. With the pretty foil wrapped outside, the new socialists believe the American people will view socialism as a valuable gift. Of course, many already view it that way by misplacing their hope in the slicing up of some pie they didn't bake.

All they can imagine is everything that's free for them on the inside. It all looks nice to the unsuspecting, but most informed adults know all too well what socialism has contributed to the world. It has brought scarcity, poverty and violence. So what is this new packaging anyway?

The enticing package of social control is an economic system without privately owned businesses. Instead, companies will be owned and controlled by the relevant stakeholders such as the workers and the community impacted by a company, hence the name social control.

I cannot use the word *business* because a business's purpose is to earn income by meeting demand. The firms in democratic socialism don't have this as their primary goal. To keep the word business from being corrupted, the words firms or enterprises will be used instead.

Ownership as well needs to be redefined. Because of private property limits of only personal effects and possibly a house, ownership means the public's stake in the control of the means of production. There will likewise be public control over some government services and the best use of natural resources.

These socially controlled firms will not exist to make as much profit as possible, but to be the tools of socialism's redistribution of resources. Those who would control the firms would primarily be the workers, but also other stakeholders such as customers, people of the community and government regulators.

At the present time, there exist similar examples of such structures. There are 300 to 400 worker cooperatives in the United States employing roughly 7,000 people.[2] The enterprises are worker owned and managed. The workers, then, vote and decide the direction of the company.

They do have to compete within a free market with businesses that have the profit motive, so it's not an exact comparison. The companies also have to provide benefits that otherwise would be provided for by the government under a socialistic system.

Up until 2020, the democratic socialism movement believed without a revolution or significant political changes, they would have to work within the current system. Co-ops are progress toward their goal, but if people can freely choose, these structures will never be able to compete with capitalism to supplant it as something better.

Since the progressives took power with Joe Biden's win over Donald Trump, social control may not even have to compete within a free market. All that will be required is simple incremental legislation.

One easy step would be to mandate that workers have seats in corporate boardrooms. This new regulation would ensure corporate revenues be allocated more equitably. Well, that sounds good. It wouldn't be immediate gratification, but this progressive step taking would surely dilute ownership stakes in corporations.

A concurrent plan is the furtherance of their power. They want to increase the likelihood of cheating in elections by having slack voting rules. Democrats also want to gain new voters through migration and to increase their representation in both houses of Congress by giving statehood to not only Washington D.C., but also Puerto Rico. Lastly, of course, is the expansion of the Supreme Court.

When they have enough political power, the progressive agenda of social control can be fully implemented. This isn't theoretical either. They are outspoken in telling us. In the next chapter under the heading *Ultimate Control*, you'll read about Elizabeth Warren's Accountable Capitalism Act that does just that.

The left is conditioning society to accept social control all the time. For example, in the fall of 2019, the United Auto Workers went on strike at General Motors. UAW Vice President Terry Dittes had many demands of GM including, "we are standing up for our share of the profits."[3]

Only in socialism are workers entitled to their share of the profits. In capitalism, shares of the profits are supposed to go to those who risked their capital investing in the company. If the company does poorly, the shareholders lose money. Are the UAW and their members willing to suffer financial loss if GM does poorly? Of course not, they just want the profits.

Joe Biden himself wanted to end what he called, "shareholder capitalism." While revealing his economic plan in July 2020, he stated his intent:[4]

> It's way past time we put an end to the era of shareholder capitalism. The idea the only responsibility a corporation has is with shareholders. That's simply not true. It's an absolute farce. They have a responsibility to their workers, their community, to their country. That isn't a new or radical notion.

Replacing Owners with Workers

The freedom to be self-reliant has come under assault in the State of California as they moved to reclassify many people to *workers*. What was once the Gold Rush State had become the Gig Crush State.

The new law has gone into effect as of 2021 and applies to persons performing a service in exchange for income.[5] The result, freelancers and gig workers will be classified as *employees* by default. Grubhub and Uber drivers, for example, will have to be considered as employees and no longer independent contractors. There are carve-outs for some industries such as doctors, securities brokers and real estate agents. It mostly affects gig economy workers and freelancers.

There was some push back by Californians. Proposition 22 was passed by the voters in the November 2020 election. A judge, however, ruled 22 was unconstitutional giving the State what it wanted. As expected, the socialists Joe Biden and Kamala Harris urged voters to defeat Proposition 22.

The State claims they are protecting freelancers and gig workers from exploitation like with low pay and zero benefits. My belief is the real reason they wanted to reclassify huge numbers of people as workers is for the eventual social control of businesses.

California is the left's proving ground and this was likely a move toward social control. As workers, they'd be economic stakeholders and eligible for wealth redistribution and other benefits. The real impact now, however, is preventing freelancers from working on their own terms.

The words *owner* and *ownership* are immoral these days in professional basketball. NBA Commissioner Adam Silver says the league is moving away from using the word owners to describe those who have ownership stakes in teams.[6] Instead they will be called *governors*. He claims it's in response to players who believe the word owner has racial overtones. The player's union, unwittingly or not, is advancing the social control ball down the court.

Democratizing Private Businesses

It wouldn't be too difficult to change our current system to one that democratizes private businesses. Imagine the city of Detroit purchasing the Detroit Pistons from the current "governor." Detroit could then structure the franchise so control is shared between the players, union, refs, other workers, fans and the city.

Such a scenario wouldn't require outright confiscation from the current owner. The city could simply sell bonds to raise money and just buy it through eminent domain. Don't be fooled, the wealth of the owner would definitely be confiscated, but humanly through a wealth tax.

Another option would be to buy the team with just a paper credit. The credit could only be used to offset future federal, state or city taxes. So then, the rich guy's inevitable taxes could be paid using his credit; win-win.

Any current business could be transformed into a public entity this way. Transitioning our free market system to a socially controlled one wouldn't be insurmountable. The only questions remaining regarding democratized firms are, would market demand go unmet and would they continually drain the taxpayers?

Because there are so many stakeholders, all with different objectives, the revenue within each firm would have severe competition. Social justice activists would be one faction who would be demanding spending. The fans or community who couldn't care less about profit or loss would have a voice too. City officials would demand crazy spending and on and on.

Even when an enterprise is running in the red, the public benefit is what would be important. The benefit would obviously be jobs and other things deemed too important to let go. That leaves the taxpayer subsidizing these entities regardless if they're meeting demand or how poorly they're run.

With the government willing to subsidize public firms for the public good, what incentive is there for these enterprises to meet market demand? If the profit motive has been removed because survival is already assured, the purpose of the enterprises would have nothing to do with meeting the needs of a marketplace to earn income. The mission statement of firms would change from promises about their brand to politically-correct lingo about equality and the social good.

Democratization wouldn't just run and ruin enterprises either. It would be extended to every area of life including government services and regulations (national and local), natural resources, energy production, city planning, banking, culture and entertainment, and any remaining philanthropic trusts and foundations. This is just partial list of the many community takeovers.

Having this entire bottom-up control by all the stakeholders would require a massive uptick in civic participation. Instead of voting every two years, everyone would have multiple ownership stakes.

It's hard to imagine myself being too geeked about attending workplace meetings, boards, town halls and assemblies all the time. If this ever comes to pass, forget about after school soccer games. We'll be too busy doing our civic duty. The old timers then, when reminiscing about the good days, will say, "When I was your age; we were free, happy and watched TV every night."

Social control policies are a central theme of democratic socialism. The advocates for the democratization of nearly everything claim it will enhance people's freedom. They also believe social control will ensure everyone takes possession of their newly granted human rights. In reality, though, the effect of democracy in everything will result in authoritarian control over all facets of society.

Authoritarianism

The democratic socialists claim their version of socialism is better than their granddaddy's kind because there's not a central authority managing society and controlling the national economy. This new kind of socialism is a democratic system placing power and control in the people's hands. This next generation of socialists still wants the benefit of equitable wealth distribution for everybody that is the utopia of socialism. They just don't want some pot-bellied two-bit dictator overseeing it all.

While it may be true that democracy is at the core of their spruced up philosophy, it's completely untrue democratic socialism is anything other than authoritarian. The reasons are because it severely restricts individual liberties and the Democratic Party will run it all. It won't be a dictator ruling by whim and whistle but rather, a system taking individual liberties away, and dictating what is acceptable and what's not.

In this new socialism, individual liberties are still subordinate to the state even though the packaging promises freedom to the masses. If the Democrats gain enough political power and implement the progressive agenda, the dismantling of our natural rights will commence.

The first to go would be the right to keep and bear arms. It may begin with so-called assault rifles, but would expand from there since small guns kill people too. They may just abolish the Second Amendment altogether or severely cripple it anyway.

John Paul Stevens, former Associate Justice on the Supreme Court (1975 to 2000) is just one example of their disdain of gun rights. He suggested in his book to amend the Second Amendment.[7] He believes we should change it by inserting the clause, "when serving in the militia." That way guns will only be allowed for military personnel.

The current 2nd says, "A well-regulated Militia, being necessary to the security of a free State, the right of the people to keep and bear Arms, shall not be infringed."

Stevens wants to change it to, "A well-regulated Militia, being necessary to the security of a free State, the right of the people to keep and bear Arms *when serving in the Militia* shall not be infringed (Emphasis added)."

Free speech would also need to be reined in. They will start by passing hate speech, nondiscriminatory and other indoctrination laws. Churches would no longer be free to fully preach God's word. Cake decorators will not be able to say "no thank you," nurses wouldn't be able to opt out of abortion procedures and parents couldn't homeschool their own kids.

From there, they'll tackle political campaign finance reform. The left wants to move away from private donors to a system of public funding. Who gets the public money? Well undoubtedly, the known commodity political elites do. That way some scurvy free marketeer populist can't sneak up on them.

This is progress for progressives, but in reality, is nothing more than authoritarianism by a political party. Currently, it would take more than laws passed by Congress to curtail much of our freedoms. If the old U.S. Constitution hasn't been scrapped by the revolutionaries yet, the Bill of Rights would still be in their way.

To bypass this obstacle, they most likely would expand the Supreme Court from nine justices to as many activist ones as it would take to allow their ideas to be constitutional. If they had sufficient political control, another option would be to just amend the Bill of Rights as needed. If progressives had the power, is any of this unlikely?

Even without changing any laws or amending the Constitution, progressives can carry out their agenda under the guise of democracy and affected stakeholders.

Think of a local church currently making decisions in-house with its leadership and members. Once it's been democratized, the outside community would have a say along with other stakeholders who are upset by church messaging and sermons. The left will contend it's democracy and bottom-up social control, but in reality it would be authoritarian through a system of a top-down politically correct culture.

Economic Tyranny

The autocratic socialists say democratic socialism isn't a dictatorship because they embrace political democracy and social control of most institutions. But what about freedom, do they embrace that?

One of the great benefits of living in a free United States is you can start a small business and become successful by meeting demand. With democratic socialism, however, you may be able to start a business, but any profits would certainly be capped.

Small businesses are only allowed to produce a livable wage for the owners; otherwise, the community would be cheated because they own the means of production. Excessive profits would necessarily revert back to the state. This is the only way the government could provide all its services to society. They would outlaw success, but tell the zombie people they're outlawing greed.

Any printed copies of this book might as well be burned. You can't create organic wealth in democratic socialism because the economic system prohibits it. In order to create organic wealth you need to save unconsumed income and then invest it.

Authoritarian democratic socialism hinders this by not allowing anyone to earn too high of an income. Even if you can save some scraps of money, depicted in blue colored socialist icons, there aren't any investment opportunities to put your bluebacks in to. They'll just lose value sitting at the bottom of your cookie jar.

With democratic socialism there isn't a stock market, investment properties, 401(k)s or other productive property where you can invest your savings. Property that's productive belongs to the public. When you can't invest saved income, organic wealth will never be more than a seed left unsprouted buried in the dirt.

Within the system of democratic socialism, there are two activities that are prohibitive to the population. They cannot engage within a free market to earn the most income possible and they're unable to invest saved income to accumulate organic wealth. Isn't that authoritarianism by a system? It's not a utopia and assuredly, it's the furthest thing away from independence.

Democratic socialism is nothing more than economic tyranny. At the time of this writing, the progressives haven't won their soft revolution yet. They're still in the mode of progressing toward this goal. To get to their authoritarian dreamland, they've concocted a pit stop at a more palatable place for the uninitialized.

They call the land of the Nordics an example of democratic socialism and say how it's so much better than dirty capitalism. In reality though, such a system would never satisfy far-left progressives because it smells too much like freedom.

Scandinavia Mania

If you look to the Scandinavians, you'll find the answers. No doubt, anyone who's witnessed a Bernie Sanders' speech has seen him wag his finger while uttering such a reference. But what kind of place is Scandinavia and are these countries examples of democratic socialism?

The Scandinavian Peninsula is made up of three countries: Denmark, Norway and Sweden. These three countries, along with Finland and Iceland, are also Nordic countries. All five are located in northern Europe and progressives say they're examples the United States should emulate.

When conservatives offer Venezuela and Cuba as examples of socialism, the left objects. The retort is those countries are not democratic and therefore not fair comparisons. They'll then point, like Bernie does, to Scandinavia and claim these places are better models.

The progressives who hate capitalism will be disappointed, however, because all the Nordic countries are capitalist. Not one country Bernie points to is socialist. This seems to be important if you're trying to sell a socialist system and claim it works elsewhere.

For that reason, it's still absolutely true to claim every time socialism has been tried, it's been a failure. Freedom lovers everywhere must reference the former USSR, Venezuela and Cuba because a successful socialist example doesn't exist.

Even though socialism's failure is factual, Scandinavian countries are examples of where the progressives want to take us, not as a final destination, but as a transformational leap forward.

Social Democracy

The Nordic countries are really examples of social democracies. The name, social democracy, isn't very descript in capturing its true essence. Every philosophy is a democracy these days, so that's understandable. The word social, though, doesn't represent socialism or social control; it represents social services.

The Nordic economies provide social benefits such as higher education, healthcare and retirement for its citizens. Unlike socialism, the economies of these countries are principally free market based and capitalist. The name doesn't capture that. Something more descriptive I would suggest is *universal capitalism*, which means universal social services on the back of capitalism.

The social benefits from these countries differ from the New Deal programs of the United States because the benefits are not just a safety net to fill the gap, but are universal for every citizen. In order to pay for it all, the citizens pay as they go with high personal taxes. Another point of difference, the Nordic countries can devote a greater percentage of their budget on these services whereas the U.S. spends 15.9% of its budget on defense.[8]

Post WWII, the goal of social democracy movements was to incrementally transform their countries from capitalist to socialist. Social democracy was their mechanism to achieve that end. They were like the 'missing link' in the theory of human evolution except the evidence of social democracies was actually in the ground and people could observe them progressing.

Instead of a violent revolution by the people to overthrow their governments, the proponents for social democracy sought a peaceful transformation by mutating their society while working within the current system. This is the strategy of many on left for the United States today.

The difference between then and now is the social democracies of the Scandinavian region aren't trying to become socialist like their forerunners generations ago; although, I'm sure there's a leftwing fraction currently who desire such a transmutation. Still, they haven't achieved nirvana yet and the work marches on to strike the right balance between a large welfare state and being able to afford it all.

Take Sweden, for instance. In 1995, Sweden's national debt to GDP was 80%, but has fallen to 41% as of 2017.[9] In the early 1990s; they had high unemployment, low economic growth, high inflation, increasing deficit spending and massive debt. Today, they have one of the highest GDPs per capita among EU nations, a balanced budget, shrinking public debt and low inflation.

Bernie's Bros should take note, turning Sweden's economy around didn't happen because of trillion dollar spending programs. Rejecting further Keynesian spending, Sweden institutionalized fiscal restraint. In 1996 they capped public spending so future growth would outpace spending resulting in a balanced budget over time. They also adopted a surplus goal, which was any state owned enterprise would have to turn a profit and not be a drain on taxpayers.

The Swedes self-describe their coalition government that rid the country of inheritance and wealth taxes as "centre–right". They tried a wealth tax from 1943 to 2007, but found the rich people just left for other countries where property rights were protected.

The next time Bernie wags his finger to over yonder, someone should ask him if he believes, like Sweden, the U.S. government should freeze spending at current levels to one day balance the budget. If he's still listening, also ask if he believes, like Sweden, that Amtrak, the U.S. Postal Service, Fannie Mae, Freddie Mac and the student loan program should be self-sufficient.

The five Nordic countries are far from democratic socialist. In actuality, they have many traits a rugged individualist would be proud of. The first separating attribute from democratic socialism is private property protections.

Private Property

The Nordic Model, also referred to as the Third Way, consists of strong private property rights. Businesses are not controlled by the workers or other stakeholders like the social control concept found in democratic socialism. They do have some employee representatives in some boardrooms, but it's the people with actual money invested who have ownership rights over company profits.

There are many more publicly owned companies compared to the United States, but most of these firms have to compete with private businesses within the free market. Hence, the managers of state-owned enterprises are similar to traditional businesses in that they have to focus on the bottom line and meet consumer demand.

According to the 2021 Index of Economic Freedom, all five of these countries rank very well and are considered 'mostly free.'[10] The report defines economic freedom as "the fundamental right of every human to control his or her own labor and property."

Denmark is ranked 10th, Iceland 11th, Finland 17th, Sweden 21st and Norway 28th. By comparison, Canada and the U.S. are ranked 9th and 20th, respectively; Mexico is 65th, which is 'moderately free'; and Singapore is ranked 1st and within the 'free' category. Switzerland, New Zealand, Ireland and Australia are also 'free.'

Taxation

To raise revenue to pay for their social services, you would think the Scandinavians would be soaking the rich. After all, in the U.S. the rich never pay their fair share so the Nordics must be good at doing that. In reality, they do have high personal taxes, but it's the middle class who are getting soaked—along with the rich.

Sweden's top marginal rate is 60.1% and applies to people who earn 1.5 times Sweden's national average income.[11] If this system was in the U.S., which had an average income of $61,937 in 2018, households earning over $92,906 would be in the top bracket and subject to a 60% federal tax rate.

Denmark's top marginal rate is 55.8% and applies to incomes that are only 1.3 times Denmark's average national income. If in the U.S., it would mean earning over just $80,518 to be subject to 55.8%.

The numbers for the other three countries: Norway 46.7%, 1.6; Iceland 44.4%, 1.2; and Finland 58.3%, 1.9. It seems in these countries, everyone pays their fair share in return for all their benefits.

In the U.S., the top bracket in 2020 was 37% for incomes over $510,301, but that's just the federal rate. On top of the federal income tax are FICA and state income taxes, which once factored with the top rate, are very comparable to the Nordic tax systems.

The federal income tax rate in the U.S. for the middle class was 22% to 24%. After adding state and FICA, they paid much less in taxes than the Nordics. If we adopted the Nordic model, they indeed would get soaked.

In addition to income taxes, the Nordics have to pay a punishing national sales tax, known as the Value Added Tax.[12] These taxes are regressive and hit the poorest the hardest because a greater portion of their income is used for consumption. The VAT rates for all five countries are either 24% or 25%.

As for the greedy corporations, the Nordic countries have low corporate tax rates.[13] The hysteria by Democrats over the corporate tax rate in the United States is misplaced. In order to compete with the rest of the world and keep jobs at home, rates had to be lowered from where they were previously at 35% to 21% under Donald Trump. The Nordic countries understand this. Their corporate tax rates are: Denmark 22%, Norway 22%, Sweden 21.4%, Finland 20% and Iceland 20%.

Freedom

The Nordic people have freedom, which they wouldn't have if they lived under democratic socialism. They are free to earn as much as they want by meeting the needs of a marketplace; they just can't keep half of it. Even though income taxes are high, it's possible to create organic wealth with unconsumed income. They are also free to invest in appreciable assets or property providing ongoing income. Societies who would embrace democratic socialism couldn't own productive property. Finally, they are free to control their property and can transfer it to others without government confiscation.

The progressives have Scandinavia mania and want the social benefits they provide. Expanding the welfare state of the United States is an ongoing debate, but unfortunately, that's not where the radical left want to stop.

Many progressives aren't satisfied with a large safety net relying on capitalism to pay for it. They want to go all the way to democratic socialism. Blame Bernie or communist college professors, but either way, the radical base is now wagging that bucking donkey.

- NINE -

Beyond Nordic

The big takeaway from the Nordic Model is the average taxpayer pays a lot in taxes for all the social services. The government in Sweden even claims their citizens enjoy paying high taxes and that the tax agency "remains pretty popular" with taxpayers.[1] It's popular notwithstanding the practical tax rate in Sweden is 52% for average salaried workers.

By applying this to their average salary of $46,804, it leaves only $22,410 in net income.[2] The Swedes then take their $22,000 and pay VAT taxes on top of their consumption. All these taxes leave little savings to create organic wealth or to splurge on a holiday to the States.

There are good reasons for the U.S. to never adopt such a model. Chiefly, the free market offers better methods to provide services such as healthcare, education and retirement. Take healthcare, for instance. There may be many things wrong with the healthcare system in the

U.S., but the greatest issue, in my opinion, is out-of-control costs. Insurance companies are vilified by the media and the left, but hospitals and other providers seem to be the greatest driver of escalating prices.

Healthcare providers deserve a bright spotlight because there's nothing that limits their ever increasing costs. Private insurance or government plans basically pay however high their prices climb. If the costs become too expensive, then insurance premiums are forced to rise.

The problem is there isn't anything constraining the demand side in the market. Healthcare is good business and it's why hospitals and clinics are popping up everywhere. If someone else is paying, people will utilize their plans without worrying about pricing. Additionally, providers will administer tests and services that may not be necessary. It all adds up to a failed market that doesn't balance supply and demand.

A market based solution restraining demand is necessary. It would be ideal if patients had skin in the game. If they had to pay a portion out of their medical savings account, they may not have that knee replacement, for example. If their medical savings account became part of their estate, they might just choose to live without jogging to instead leave the money to their children.

Other necessary ways to check demand would be price transparency and determining testing or treatment needs that's not influenced by a provider's profit motive. The latter requires patients being price conscious.

It's the free market that has the answers. Just like free healthcare, free college doesn't constrain the demand side. The same is true of college loans. Again, students need to have real skin in the game which would place a check on their demand. If students' demand included price, the supply would work to satisfy that demand.

College savings plans that are not utilized should be distributed back to the student without a tax penalty. We just need to figure out a way for parents to begin saving.

As for retirement, again the free market is the answer. By creating organic wealth over a lifetime, it would negate the need for a large safety net. If we're going to force people into something, we should start by forcing them into saving a portion of their income.

Yes, I'm calling for forced savings that the government can't touch! I know this seems anti-freedom, but we're taxing workers and businesses FICA already. Rather than paying into a Ponzi scheme like FICA, we should be putting that 15.3% of gross income into an account that each of us own. Additional contributions could be made also. This would ultimately lessen the burden on society, reduce the size of government and allow market based solutions for our greatest challenges.

The account would be for each employee's retirement, healthcare and children's college. We could call it the *Savings Tax*. The amount wouldn't go to the U.S. Treasury but directly into a government regulated account the taxpayer owns. It would then be managed by a private investment company. Whatever's not used within a taxpayer's lifetime would become a part of their estate.

I believe Chief Justice John Roberts would be okay with it as long as we call it an indirect tax. Even better, if the States ratified the Organic Wealth Amendment, this savings tax would be a direct tax not needing apportionment because it would be on income. And, no estate taxes too.

Instead of relying on the free market, however, there are some Democrats who would favor the U.S. to switch to a version of the Nordic Model. Many progressives, though, see the Nordic Model as some sort of half-chimp, half-man transitional creature that should eventually be left behind for sociologists to one day study.

These progressives, who also possess all the energy in the Democratic Party, want to go beyond the Nordics to full-fledged democratic socialism. How do we know that? Well, those who ran in the 2020 Democratic presidential primaries told us so. Thus, reflecting the progressive base's policy demands.

Ultimate Control

The Democratic Party has changed considerably in recent years. They were once known for their tax-and-spend plans that resulted in a large safety net, which Rush Limbaugh used to call a hammock. Republicans would resist their ideas advocating for lower taxes and personal responsibility instead. That was the national debate and we mostly met somewhere in the middle.

As of the 2020 elections, the Democrats still want a safety net, but are pushing for much more. Even now many point to Scandinavia as some kind of paradise, but that's not what they're really advocating for. Their policy proposals betray them. It seems what they're really aiming at is democratic socialism.

As described in the previous chapter, social control in democratic socialism is partly defined as when the workers control the means of production. Many on the left are zeroing in on America's most prosperous businesses in steps toward such a goal.

Senator Elizabeth Warren's *Accountable Capitalism Act*, for instance, would transform the purpose of the largest corporations in the United States. They would no longer be principally for-profit, but instead, they'll essentially be handed over to the workers. As you'll see, this isn't the Nordic Model but rather, socialistic.

In order to enact her policies, she has to sell the problem which according to her, is that corporate profits go to the shareholders. Instead, she would like to see profits go to business investment by hiring more workers or go directly to the workers with higher wages. Warren's press release about the act quotes her saying:[3]

> There's a fundamental problem with our economy. For decades, American workers have helped create record corporate profits but have seen their wages hardly budge. To fix this problem we need to end the harmful corporate obsession with

> maximizing shareholder returns at all costs, which has sucked trillions of dollars away from workers and necessary long-term investments.

Her bill has five provisions. First, she would require both public and private corporations with revenues over one billion to obtain a federal charter as a *United States Corporation.* The charter would obligate these corporations to "consider the interests of all corporate stakeholders - including employees, customers, shareholders, and the communities in which the company operates."

Without having this charter, a billion dollar corporation couldn't legally operate within the United States. More importantly, another of her provisions would place a corporation's charter in jeopardy if it engaged in illegal activity, which would include not considering all the interests of every stakeholder. This type of strong arming would fundamentally change how corporations are run.

If the government determines corporate board members did not correctly consider some stakeholder's interest, the corporation could lose its federal charter. This places immense pressure and liability on board members, which would change the purpose of a corporation. The current model is to meet the needs of a marketplace for the purpose of earning as much profit as possible. After Warren's plan, the model would change so a corporation's existence is mostly for the public good.

Senator Warren claims this idea is based on the relatively new *benefit corporation.*[4] B-corps are similar to regular

C-corps, but allow a corporation to provide a social benefit instead of being legally obligated to maximize shareholder profits. Benefit corporations may be chartered in thirty-six states with more coming.

The difference between B-corps and Warren's plan is benefit corporations have a specific social benefit, and it's completely optional for a business in these states to form this structure. In Warren's plan, corporations must take into account the social benefits of all the stakeholders and it's mandatory.

Warren's plan shapes up to be very similar to *social control* within democratic socialism. The only difference is she leaves shareholders as one of the stakeholders. After such legislation, though, these shareholders would be the ones who get left holding the bag. The stock price would plummet with this type of mandatory reordering of a corporation's purpose.

The stock price would plummet because profits would decline precipitously. Revenues would need to be spent toward fulfilling their mission as a public good enterprise instead of maximizing profit. In other words, profits would go extinct because revenue would be diverted for other stakeholder interests. The value known today would be gone forever.

A third provision of her bill would mandate the corporate boards of all federally chartered United States Corporations be made up of 40% of employees. So for every five members of a board, two of those five would be required to be made up of employee representatives. Requiring 40% employee representation places employees in the driver's seat so that one day they'll be in nearly complete control of these chartered corporations.

Mandating 40% employee representatives would effectively be the same as unionizing all the employees of the largest companies in America. It would just be much more powerful. Instead of just negotiating employee benefits and wages, the employee board seats allows a negotiation over every aspect of how a company is run.

Given the directive of the federal charter that all stakeholders' interests must be considered, having a board composed of 40% employees would give the employee contingent almost complete power. All that these employee seats would need on a board of five is for one of the non-employee members to vote in their favor.

Accomplishing this type of dominance in voting would be quite easy for the employee faction because of the federal mandate to take into account all the stakeholders' interests, and considering the next step in her plan.

Her bill would also restrict board members and officers from selling their shares of stock for a number of years. This type of restriction, along with the previous steps, would change how officers and board members are compensated. Their compensation would change from stock options to some other form such as cash bonuses and higher salaries because company stock wouldn't be attractive any longer.

With board members being compensated without stock, who would be in the boardroom advocating for the interests of the shareholders? The three non-employee members have to consider every stakeholder's interests, which only partly include shareholders. Having two seats on the board and only having to convince one other to turn their way will over time give the employees of the corporation more power and ultimate control.

The last item in her bill is about restricting political contributions from corporations. To do so, it would require 75% approval from shareholders and 75% approval from the board. This is to ensure corporations cannot lobby Congress to revoke her act. A board of five requires four members allowing the expenditure, which would never happen given the employees controlling 40% of the seats.

Senator Warren's Act would affect both public and private corporations having revenues over $1 billion. According to Fortune 500, the top 1,000 companies in the U.S. all have revenues exceeding or near $2 billion, which would require them to transition to a federally chartered corporation under Warren's plan.[5]

This means most of America's successful companies would have their purpose transformed from meeting demand and maximizing profit to some conception of public good. Once that's accomplished, what would stop all smaller corporations from suffering the same fate?

It's not just Warren's plan either. Kamala Harris as Senator in 2018 joined Warren (D-MA), Booker (D-NJ), Gillibrand (D-NY), Sanders (I-VT) and eight other Senators in a letter to the SEC's chairperson.[6] They wanted the SEC's Staff Roundtable to adopt worker representation on corporate boards. Workers are investors too?

> We strongly believe meaningful ownership can and should be determined by the value of contributions made to the company by its various stakeholders. Workers, for example, invest their time, skill, and effort in the company, and—like shareholders—depend on managers to both generate a return on that investment and share that return in the form of increased compensation.

Many cite Germany's codetermination laws as an example the U.S. should follow. Their system for large public corporations allows workers to elect from one-third up to one-half of board members of the *supervisory board*, depending on the company's size.

In Germany, however, corporations must be comprised of two boards, management and supervisory. The codetermination by workers applies only to the supervisory board, but not the management board. The U.S. doesn't have such a mandatory split of different boards. There is only one corporate board, so the worker faction in the U.S. would be much more powerful.

Guaranteed Job

In a socialistic economy there will be a job for everyone, guaranteed. It arises from the belief that in socialism society owns the wealth and the means of production. For there to be economic justice, therefore, any revenue created must be distributed equitably. With a view to achieve this outcome, employment is provided for all who are able to work. Those then who are unable to be employed will just be provided a paycheck.

The aspiring democratic socialists of today have many avenues to distribute the loot they confiscate. They can create government jobs in the public sector, spend money in the private sector, pay unemployment compensation, give social welfare for those who cannot work, and pass out a universal basic income.

In 2021, Biden called for spending trillions of dollars in the private sector on so-called infrastructure, COVID relief, and other bills; which were primarily for leftist agenda items. Allocating this money picks winners in our economy, which does create jobs, but it also picks losers.

The job losses from abhorred industries such as non-renewable energy aren't mentioned in the bills beyond designating billions to retrain displaced workers. If we're referring to democratic socialism, we can't talk about central planning because it doesn't exist, so shhh!

Historically, Democrats favored public sector jobs to ensure they had many employees who had a financial interest in keeping the spigot open. If these workers wanted to keep the good times rolling, they'd be sure to vote Democratic. The matter of contention with these jobs is they produce nothing of value for any market.

Whether the government spends money in the public or private sectors, it's mere mortal bureaucrats who decide which jobs to develop. This, of course, is the problem. The fatal flaw is that the supply side isn't working to satisfy demand. Therefore, demand goes unmet and private capital is diverted to industries that are not meeting customer needs and desires.

There are many progressives who now want the government to become the employer of last resort. This would mean that if a person couldn't find a job in the private sector, they could always become a government employee regardless of skill level or competence.

As we'll see, many leaders in the Democratic Party are in favor of a federal job guarantee program and not just spending in the private sector. They list industries such as construction, healthcare, senior care or environmental where they would like to make government jobs.

As a consequence of these unlimited federal jobs, if anyone doesn't like their career in the private sector, they can work for the public sector instead. And why wouldn't many make the switch to obtain a good living wage with full benefits and job security?

A job guarantee program is not the Scandinavian way, however. There would be many negatives such as it would cost too much, thwart marketplace demand, and it would jeopardize their other social programs. Lastly, guaranteeing jobs would place the private sector under tremendous pressure.

With a federal jobs program, businesses will have to compete for workers who could otherwise have guaranteed government careers. This non-market force will artificially inflate private sector wages. We got a sense of labor shortages and artificially higher wages when people were paid more to stay home than to work because of the extra federal unemployment paid out during COVID-19.

A guaranteed jobs program will increase the costs for businesses and will further squeeze their budgets resulting in unmet demand and less jobs. This will obviously give the public sector many more workers.

Before long, businesses won't be able to hire the necessary talent to meet demand. As a result and because of higher employee costs, profits will decline; thus, creating less tax revenue. This will place pressure on the federal government's budget, which would have a world of obligations. Guaranteeing jobs will be one reason why their equitable distribution of wealth turns into poverty for all.

The Nordics don't have guaranteed jobs because that would be a tenet of socialism and not social democracy. So you would think the stars of the Democratic Party would stop short of supporting such policies. Unfortunately, though, they're showing us what they really want with their socialistic proposals.

AOC's Green New Deal

Alexandria Ocasio-Cortez made headlines by introducing the Green New Deal in February 2019.[7] The bill, nevertheless, has many resolutions that don't have anything to do with climate change. One of resolutions not only guarantees high wage jobs but also ensures economic prosperity for everyone. The clause commits to "create millions of good, high-wage jobs and ensure prosperity and economic security for all people of the United States."

Another of AOC's resolutions within the Green New Deal promises full benefits and retirement security along with a guaranteed job for everyone that provides a living wage for families. The clause states, "Guaranteeing a job with a family-sustaining wage, adequate family and medical leave, paid vacations, and retirement security to all people of the United States."

You might think such a socialist job guarantee comes only from a former bartender who's idealistic and wears rose-colored glasses. But this House bill had 95 Democratic cosponsors. There is a Senate version too that's exactly the same and was introduced by Ed Markey (D-MA).[8] That bill had 14 Democratic cosponsors including former presidential candidates: Cory Booker (D-NJ), Amy Klobuchar (D-MN), Bernie Sanders (I-VT), Kirsten Gillibrand (D-NY), and Elizabeth Warren (D-MA). It was also cosponsored by Biden's eventual Vice President pick, Kamala Harris (D-CA).

The House bill wasn't put to vote so we have no idea if the entire Democratic caucus would have supported this fundamental principle of socialism. The Senate bill was forced to the floor by Republicans, but was defeated 57-0 with most Democrats chickening out and voting *present.*[9]

Other Job Ideas

The Green New Deal is supported whole-heartedly by Bernie Sanders. In his *Jobs for All* policy on his website, he says, "As part of the Green New Deal, we need millions of workers to rebuild our crumbling infrastructure."[10] He also lists two other areas where we'll need jobs: education and senior care.

Bernie doesn't say what would happen if his worker bees have no interest in working construction, educating kids, or in helping seniors. We can only assume there will be other made up jobs equivalent to sweeping streets or shoveling paper. We know, after all, what it will actually be doing, which is redirecting otherwise productive capital over to consumption.

Some candidates from the Democratic presidential primary supported Senator Cory Booker's guaranteed job program.[11] He introduced legislation for a three year pilot program to guarantee federal jobs starting at $15 an hour with full benefits. If passed, it would be tested in fifteen high unemployment communities. The bill was co-sponsored by presidential candidates: Kirsten Gillibrand, Kamala Harris and Elizabeth Warren.

Universal Basic Income

A similar idea to guaranteeing jobs is a universal basic income (UBI). Andrew Yang proposed giving $1,000 per month to everyone living in America who are eighteen years and older.[12] The money would be deposited every month no matter if the person had a job or not. The price tag was only $3 trillion a year. It seems to me people would feel more secure if it were $3,000 per month. If we can spend $3 trillion on a universal basic income program, then why not spend $9 trillion?

Mark Zuckerberg of Facebook supports some sort of UBI. So does Elon Musk of Tesla. The reason they agree with Yang regarding UBI is because they all believe automation will soon take away people's jobs.

But Yang says on his website the benefits from UBI are everything from improving mental and physical health to reducing violence. We shouldn't be fooled by all this. The answer to automation and a robot named Carl is meeting the needs of the marketplace which may require using or obtaining a different skill.

If you can remember back before modernism, there once were bookkeepers who used pencils and paper every day. These accountants, along with every business in existence, had to use paper-based systems to keep track of every transaction and record. Companies would devote massive storage space to house their data sets.

I'm sure if the fear mongers back then knew computers and software would be able to accomplish basic tasks 10,000 times faster and with perfect accuracy, they would have also shouted doom and gloom. The fact is more jobs were created around computers and IT than were otherwise lost. And as a result of new technology, productivity improved demonstrably.

The real intent of UBI programs is to redistribute wealth, creating government dependents out of as much people as possible. The more who depend upon the government for their income, the easier it will be to implement the left's takedown of capitalism in favor of democratic socialism. A basic income is nothing more than the start of equitable wealth distribution found in socialism.

There are several American cities that began implementing a UBI in 2021 with some programs that are just for minorities of color, so maybe not universal. There are also Democrats who are proposing a permanent child tax credit that the IRS would pay out monthly. The city plans are tests so we'll have to see if people are lifted out of their circumstance when work is disincentivized.

As for the Nordics, Finland finished an experimental program with UBI and reported its results in October 2019.[13] It gave 560 euros every month to 2,000 unemployed people from January 2017 to December 2018. As it turns out, the recipients really loved the program, but researchers found the money didn't help the unemployed find a job any better than those who didn't receive a monthly check. The government of Finland has decided not to expand the program.

Economic Equality

A wealth tax for the purpose of economic equality is a democratic socialism attribute and not a Nordic one. The progressives who point to the wealth gap as evidence of unjust distribution aren't seeking to build wealth for those who don't have any. That notion doesn't even cross their minds. It seems their intention is just to dismantle the wealth accumulation from those who have earned it.

As I've pointed out many times in this book, wealth is not distributed, but is created by meeting market demand. People who have obtained wealth didn't prevent anyone else from obtaining their own. We can all create organic wealth by simply fulfilling demand and then saving our income.

In socialism, anything of value belongs to the members of society. This would include most real estate, with the possible exception of personal residences; all natural resources; property that stores value; productive property, which are assets that produce income; and any enterprise contributing to the nation's economic output. As a consequence, any revenue derived from these assets belongs to the people. This is how a theoretical socialist economy would operate.

The United States is a functioning capitalist system, though, where there are private property rights and a free market. In our system, people are incentivized to meet demand to earn as much income as possible. So without a violent revolution causing millions to die in the streets, how would revolutionaries transform capitalism to a community based economy?

To do so peacefully, the socialist wannabees would attack our system on several fronts. I've already shared two in this chapter: giving the workers ultimate control and having a guaranteed federal jobs program. The end game is to transfer the control of the means of production to the workers and away from owners. Most importantly, a key element will be to make every person in the country an economic stakeholder.

When each resident is an economic stakeholder, everybody can share in the country's prosperity. What's needed next is a way to level the playing field so there's equal prosperity and equal access to social services.

To level the playing field, the rich need a good *stick 'em up* or someone needs to turn them upside down to shake their pockets loose. First, the government would need to rob the rich with a wealth tax. They wouldn't take it all at once. They would start by making a wealth tax lawful and then only the most excessive would be grabbed. Second, the government would hinder people's ability to accumulate additional wealth with a steep progressive income tax. The highest bracket would be 70% or higher.

In order to pass these new tax laws, they have to convince the public the government should provide free healthcare, college and other necessities to ensure human rights. They would also have substantial climate change investments. With all these new government expenditures, not to mention our current deficit spending, taxes will necessarily go up. This will be the predicate for going after high income earners and those with wealth.

Once you have the mechanisms for existing wealth to be confiscated and you're blocking further wealth from being accumulated, you're basically halfway there. You can let father time take the wealth away or increase the expenditures of the government to create another predicate to increase the rate of confiscation.

Succeeding on these fronts may not be exactly textbook democratic socialism, but you would be really close. To progress toward the actual dream, screws would need to be tightened. The next step would be a 100% tax bracket to prevent earning too high of an income. Another would be prohibiting the ownership of productive property with the possible exception of a very small business. The goal would be to get to a place where everyone has a fair income so there are no longer poor people or rich people. There would be some cleaning up to do to achieve a working democratic socialism model, but the job would no longer be an overhaul.

Wealth Tax Plans

The progressive base wants a wealth tax and had top-tier candidates who were willing to do their bidding. They were, of course, Bernie Sanders and Elizabeth Warren. Other Democratic primary candidates supported a wealth tax too: Tom Steyer and New York City Mayor Bill de Blasio (D).[14] Both couldn't garner much support and were never really contenders for the nomination.

Under the Bernie Sanders' plan, which he calls a "Tax on extreme wealth," he has the following annual wealth tax rates for married couples.[15] For single people, the asset values would be halved.

1% on assets valued between $32 million and 50 million

2% on assets $50 million to $250 million

3% on assets $250 million to $500 million

4% on assets $500 million to $1 billion

5% on assets $1 billion to $2.5 billion

6% on assets $2.5 billion to $5 billion

7% on assets $5 billion to $10 billion

8% on assets over $10 billion

Let's look at an example of an ultra-rich couple who have $20 billion in wealth. Year one, the wealth tax owed would be $1.4 billion. Year two, it would be a little less than $1.4 billion since their assets' value would have dropped from the previous year's tax. The reason their asset's value drops is that the rate of accumulation would be far less than the rate of taxation.

Bernie's website claims after 15 years, the wealth of billionaires would be cut in half. He also maintains billionaires shouldn't even exist so we should expect over time they wouldn't.[16] Once the billionaires are gone, would the Democrats have the super millionaires in their sights for extinction? Who would be next after they've picked pocketed all the regular millionaires?

Elizabeth Warren's pre-election plan had only two brackets for an annual wealth tax: 2% on assets $50 million to $1 billion and 3% on assets over $1 billion.[17] When she released her $52 trillion Medicare for all plan,[18] it included an additional 3% of wealth taxes on assets worth over $1 billion for a total of 6%. Her plan also raises $trillions by taxing paper capital gains and transactions for securities. Warren would've also raised taxes on corporations, personal income and capital gains.

Warren states on her website the reason we need a wealth tax is that the income tax isn't sufficient in taxing the rich because their actual income for the year could be insignificant. That's a terrible justification because wealth is accumulated from after-tax earnings or gains. It's what's left over from already being taxed.

Warren claimed her wealth tax would have confiscated $3 trillion over ten years. The revenue was to go toward any number of her plans: Medicare for All, free college and student debt relief, among other things.

In March 2021, Warren reintroduced a wealth tax plan called the Ultra-Millionaire Tax Act.[19] It would tax 2% annually on the wealth of households and trusts between $50 million and $1 billion. For households and trusts over $1 billion, they would pay 3% annually.

This time her plan was cosponsored by seven senators including Bernie Sanders (I-VT), Kirsten Gillibrand (D-NY), Edward Markey (D-MA), and Mazie Hirono (D-HI). It was also cosponsored by House members including Pramila Jayapal (D-WA) and Brendan Boyle (D-PA). As of the writing of this book, Joe Biden or Kamala Harris hadn't endorsed her or any wealth tax plan yet.

The question for both Sanders and Warren is what will they do when the money raised over ten years is spent and the rich's wealth declines? How would the programs be funded in another decade with less wealth tax revenue coming in? The answer has to be deeper confiscation in an unending downward cycle. When wealth is taxed more than it can accumulate, the initial tax rates and brackets will be insufficient in maintaining tax revenue.

Taxing wealth is said to be for the purpose of providing free social services like healthcare, higher education and so much more. But it's also for the purpose of economic equality. Holding up the rich for economic fairness is why democratic socialism is the real Democratic Party objective and not the Nordic Model as many claim.

Open Borders

The progressive base had at least two candidates running in the 2020 election who wanted to institutionalize the mechanisms that could bring us closer to democratic socialism. The group of voters who would support overhauling American capitalism, or remake it as Elizabeth Warren would say, is pretty significant. On October 24, 2019 the Quinnipiac poll had Warren at 28% and Bernie Sanders at 15% of Democratic primary voters.[20] That's 43% of Democratic primary voters who supported either a *socialist* or Bernie Sanders.

While the number is substantial, it's doubtful the rest of the country would be interested in remaking America. If it were 43% of the total electorate, then candidate Joe

Biden wouldn't have pretended to be some moderate unifier from Scranton. He would have revealed his true progressive intentions every day to all who would listen. Instead, he hid in his basement with his mask on.

Since general election voters weren't interested in democratic socialism and probably never will be, the Democrats would like to bring in other more responsive voters. They won't admit this out loud, but it seems to be the reason why they were against President Trump's immigration policies when he was in office. They weren't just against one aspect, but against everything he wanted to do.

Democrats no longer wanted to build a southern border wall and resisted Donald Trump's efforts every step of the way. Beto O'Rourke, in fact, said he would take down existing border wall sections and claimed the wall didn't make El Paso any safer.[21]

Many of the Democratic primary candidates supported decriminalizing illegal border crossings with no more deportations. They instead wanted to make illegal crossings just a civil infraction. Those in favor: Julián Castro, Cory Booker, Pete Buttigieg, Elizabeth Warren, Bernie Sanders, and Kamala Harris.[22]

When the Biden Administration took over, they immediately reversed all of Trump's successful illegal immigration policies. They halted the construction of the border wall; ended remain in Mexico; ceased issuing deportations; tore up *safe third country agreements* with Mexico, Guatemala, El Salvador, and Honduras; and reinstated catch and release. They did keep children in cages, however. Their new policies told the world the gate in the wall was wide open and it had a welcome mat.

Today's Democratic Party doesn't want any restriction on asylum seekers whether or not they're seeking safety or just an economic opportunity. With Trump, they misrepresented protecting children from non-family adults as "separating children from their parents." They also falsely claimed the Trump Administration was putting children in cages. AOC made a run to the border and said Homeland Security was making detainees drink from the toilet. These false charges only served to undermine the Border Patrol's efforts to protect our southern border.

Not only did they reverse Trump's illegal immigration policies, but they also created magnets for more people to migrate north. Where else in the world could you illegally enter, be protected from deportation, get a good job without paying federal income taxes, have an anchor baby, access a range of public services, and one day be rewarded with citizenship?

The left wants to attract as many people as possible from countries south of the U.S. or from anywhere else. This is especially true if they're poor and uneducated. It doesn't matter as long as they'd be susceptible to socialistic policies. If the Democrats can get them here, they know eventually they'll have a massive voter base.

Along with having strong magnets to attract illegals, many within the Democratic Party would put an end to

Immigration and Customs Enforcement (ICE). The abolish ICE movement came to national prominence in 2018 with support from AOC, Kamala Harris and Elizabeth Warren. Harris didn't say abolish, but she came close by saying ICE needed reexamined and "we need to probably think about starting from scratch."[23]

The abolish ICE movement isn't popular among moderates or conservatives. Therefore, the Democratic presidential hopefuls had more palatable stances on ICE. They would keep the agency, but reform it by limiting their ability to deport anyone here illegally.

In the end, the Democrats would like the twenty million plus illegals to remain in the country permanently so one day they'll become legal residents and members of their party. Most of the 2020 primary candidates supported a pathway to citizenship, including Joe Biden. As President, Biden wanted an eight year pathway for illegals to become citizens so they can vote blue legally.

Not the Nordic Way

Liberal open border policies are nothing like those in Scandinavia. The Nordic countries are famous for their welfare state, but with all the expensive government benefits there's also a social contract.

It's expected able-bodied people will get trained for a career so they may support themselves and not be a burden on society. For this reason, there are limits on accepting new migrants and asylum seekers.

As a result of the 2015 Syrian and Afghanistan migrant crisis, many sought asylum in Scandinavia. Sweden, for example, took in a record 160,000 asylum seekers;[24] the most per capita in Europe.

Even though Nordic countries were generous by accepting those fleeing war-torn areas, it was an orderly and legal process to apply and become a legal resident. To say it differently, a Swedish political party didn't encourage millions of people to break Sweden's immigration laws so liberals could have more voters.

The Nordic countries have some of the highest personal taxes in the world. In order for their welfare states to function, they can't have unlimited amounts of migrants entering their countries and taking advantage of all the social services. It would be a breakdown of their social contract and their governments would go bankrupt. The logical conclusion: you can't have both open borders and universal welfare.

If the Democrats were actually only interested in welfare services like the Nordics have, then they wouldn't be for open borders. They would be advocating for tight borders instead. They would only want to allow in true asylum seekers and meritorious migrants who would add to our economy and not be a drain.

Limited immigration is the only responsible way to advocate for free healthcare, college, a basic income and all the rest. Otherwise, the welfare system will become overburdened and it will lead to the bankruptcy of the country. It's irresponsible for an entire political party to be for open borders and free anything.

When asked in a MSNBC primary debate if their government healthcare plan "would provide coverage for undocumented immigrants," all the candidates on the stage raised their hands including Joe Biden, Bernie Sanders, Pete Buttigieg, Kamala Harris and Andrew Yang.[25]

It was no surprise that Bernie raised his hand. He supports economic human rights, which includes a living wage of at least $15 per hour, free college and free healthcare.[26] It's only reasonable, if these things are human rights, they would be extended to everyone no matter their immigration status.

Since it's illogical to be for essentially open borders and universal welfare for everyone, it makes one wonder if there's not an ulterior motive. Could it be they see millions of undocumented immigrants as their ticket for electoral success in the future? Never mind the greatest promise of America is freedom. Democrats would promise the world at our doorstep free things instead.

The progressives' open border policy stances are not about human rights because coupled with Nordic universal welfare, those policies will bankrupt the country. Then, everybody would suffer.

The left also doesn't talk about a social contract where members of society are expected to obtain a marketable skill so they can support themselves and not be a burden. They actually appear to rather support the dependency of residents upon the government. It's why they want a permanent child tax credit paid out monthly, federal unemployment that exceeds what one may earn with a job, a universal basic income, and on and on.

In my opinion, what the left is really after are voters who will support the remaking of America from capitalism to a form of democratic socialism. They need such voters to cancel out votes from citizens who don't want to abandon free markets and organic wealth creation.

If progressives reach their destination, then democratic socialism will uproot the climate that allows organic wealth creation. The things we take for granted like private property rights, free markets, investment opportunities and other personal freedoms will be gone.

Democratic socialism wouldn't be the promised paradise that many college educated millennials believe it to be. On the contrary, the wealth pie would stop expanding and begin shrinking. There will be much less to divvy up than what's imagined due to wealth in democratic socialism becoming a zero sum game.

- TEN -

Zero Sum Wealth

When a population embraces socialism, the wealth of that population becomes zero sum. In the fifth chapter, private property was stated to be paramount to capitalism's success. Private property rights incentivize all of us to bring something of value to a marketplace to compete for income whether it's from employment or entrepreneurship. This competition for property not only increases income for each of us, but everyone's standard of living improves throughout society. It improves because a competitive marketplace unleashes productivity, inventions, innovations and greater access to all of it by every economic class.

This is the reason why free-market capitalists rightly oppose any notion of socialism. If it's true Democrats have veered so far left they're now embracing socialist ideas, then our entire system is in jeopardy. The two political parties have always agreed on our economic system of capitalism. Having this common denominator has made

America the most prosperous nation of all time. That may change if China continues to embrace free markets.

True socialists believe existing wealth belongs to everyone in society. They don't believe there should be different economic classes. Therefore, profits from an enterprise belong to society as a whole for redistribution as needed. It doesn't belong to individuals, shareholders or business owners.

Workers do receive a paycheck, but there's no incentive to bring something of value to a marketplace because there's no opportunity to increase income. When you begin redistributing wealth, you remove the private property incentive away from the recipients of that wealth. They no longer have the motivation to bring something of value to a market to obtain the most income possible.

Socialist policies that provide a guaranteed job or a UBI, plus tons of other social benefits, make wealth closer to zero sum. When you take existing wealth away from one person to give to another person or group, you are removing capital that would otherwise be deployed to produce things of value. Instead, the recipients just consume that capital. Therefore, redistributing wealth impairs future wealth creation while at the same time it decreases the size of the wealth pie.

The receivers of this wealth are not exchanging something of equal value for it in a transaction. They just obtain benefits or money, but not by satisfying demand. By removing the motive to create income, vast numbers of people will become complacent and unproductive and won't add any economic value to our economy.

Productivity will decrease; inventions, innovations and disruptions within industries will not happen. As a result, our standard of living will plateau and even decline. What made the U.S. economy the best in the world will be overtaken by an upsurging China that's embraced free markets, though the government is a dictatorship.

Barren Land

The environmentalists are sort of correct, there really is a crisis looming ahead. If we don't do something and Democrats win more elections, strengthening their political power, then organic wealth will soon cease to exist. This would be catastrophic to our economy and for our standard of living. Something must be done!

We would never want to live in a country that's become barren. In such a place nothing can grow and what had previously grown will begin dying until it's eventually dust. There's no growth because the environment doesn't allow for it. Just like a cottonwood seed planted in desert sands will not sprout, so likewise any seeds planted in AOC's America won't turn into anything either.

A barren land is the opposite of free market capitalism, which allows organic wealth creation. Even if you have some seeds, such as cash money, there's no fertile soil to plant them in to create a harvest of new wealth. As a matter of fact, money will decrease in value with any inflation caused by the Keynesians at the helm. So naturally, it becomes a hot potato until it's consumed.

The first environmental problem is limiting the income someone may earn. Adhering to the principle of *equality* found in democratic socialism, individuals cannot earn too high of an income. There still may be different economic classes based on contribution, but that's not the ideal. In order to prevent an out of control income gap, incomes would have a limit for equality's sake.

In the U.S's version of democratic socialism, it would mean a top tax bracket of 100%. They could accomplish it another way by having a top tax bracket of less than 100%, but then having a robust wealth tax, which would prevent wealth from accumulating too much.

In order for everyone's income to be fair, most people would be classified as a worker. There may be small business owners, but the amount they could profit would also be capped. So if little Jimmy found a way to sell millions of widgets online, any profit exceeding the allowable limit would be taken with a 100% tax bracket. Sorry Jimmy. The goal of socialism is equal outcomes so unchecked income generation is prohibited.

Limiting income will contribute to the land becoming barren. As a result of such hindrance, most people will just consume their income and leave nothing left over as savings. Why would anyone need to save much anyway when healthcare, higher education and even retirement are free government benefits?

Even if you recall the sage advice from radio financial expert Dave Ramsey to sacrifice today so "later you can live like no one else," it won't matter much.[1] What would be the point of sacrificing? You could sock some away for a future vacation or to buy a big ticket item, which will depreciate. That would be nice, yes, but that's about it.

The only value of saved income in a barren land is future consumption. If you're not willing to risk inflation eating it away, it would be better to consume it before too long. Forget about building wealth. That's a no-no.

Wealth building is outlawed because private property rights aren't what they used to be. The only property individuals will be able to own is personal property. For example; an automobile to get to your job to support the community, clothes to cover your nakedness, a boat for your hobby so you don't kill anybody, and a house to scream privately to God's ears. Productive property and other assets would be prohibited. Power to the people!

Productive and Non-Productive Assets

So back in the day, you graduated from Financial Peace University where you learned about saving.[2] Good on you. The problem, penny pincher, is with democratic socialism there are zero investment opportunities to grow your money. That's the next environmental issue we need to take seriously.

There will be no 401(k) to invest in or even stocks to buy with an investment account because the stock market will no longer exist. The reason is because there won't be corporations organized as they are presently with purchasable shares. That will be done away with. In its place are enterprises that are publicly owned. If an entity is profitable, the profits will go toward other things like worker pay or over to the government to pay out benefits. It will not go to owners or shareholders because corporate ownership will not survive the revolution.

So where can you put your money to earn interest or for appreciation? The only place is the bank for future consumption. That's it. There will not be the ability to invest in non-productive or productive assets. Non-productive assets don't produce income, but may increase in value over time. Examples would be gold, vacant land or a painting by Vincent van Gogh.

While you may be able to buy a house, profiting from its future sale would be considered income and subject to income limitations. Forget about the Van Gogh worth millions. That will belong to the public and will hang in a museum somewhere. Owing assets of too much value would be considered non-personal and subject to some wealth tax so that the American community remains just.

Also banned will be productive property assets, which produce income. Examples would be an ownership stake in a business, rental properties, intellectual property that pays royalties, and bonds. Individuals and groups of people cannot own productive property because revenue production, i.e., the means of production, belongs to all of society and not private individuals anymore.

Replacing Incentive

With a capitalist system, the free market is what drives production. The power behind that drive is the incentive to earn the most income as possible. That incentive results in new inventions and innovations making life more enjoyable and easier for everyone. This would include those earning the least. But the socialists would forbid people from acting on such a motivation.

They believe the competitive marketplace in capitalism overproduces resulting in booms and bust cycles, which wastes resources. Democratic socialists want to remove profit from being the motivator that leads to the production of goods and services. In its place, they envision a planned economy where the production of goods and services is managed by stakeholders who will determine output. I.e., rather than having GM produce many kinds of cars for a diverse market, the stakeholders will just produce enough unvarying electric cars as needed.

The removal of the incentive to earn an income is the greatest crime against the environment. It's not just an attack against rich soil, which holds the potential to produce an unlimited amount of wealth, but it additionally attacks human nature itself.

Demand Deficient

Socialism not only makes the land barren, but it removes another necessary element for a prosperous nation, the force of market demand. When an economy becomes demand deficient, it means there's no need to satisfy the customer as a prerequisite to obtaining income. This is the complete opposite of how a free market economy functions where supply works to satisfy demand in order to earn an income, S ▷ D.

The reason income *isn't* dependent upon satisfying demand is that in socialism, income is guaranteed. Since society owns the means of production, income from production is a fundamental right of all. Therefore, income is distributed in the form of a paycheck or a guaranteed job. It's not from meeting demand in the marketplace.

A guaranteed income is why a socialist society isn't incentivized to meet demand. People will not have the need to strive to bring value to a market in the hopes of exchanging it for income. This will make the marketplace inefficient and leave the demand side unsatisfied.

You may think since a government paycheck would be pretty basic, there would be the motivation to meet demand to earn more than what's offered as a guaranteed income. But doing so wouldn't be an option because the government would place limits on how much income someone would be allowed to earn. By removing the possibility for people to be successful and prosperous, the demand side would remain unmet.

Planned Economy

The only hope for the demand side is for stakeholders or the government to somehow learn what would be desired or needed and then to act on that information. Basically, the consumer is beholden to central planners who have no personal reason to produce anything. There isn't any financial gain enticing them, but only real budget pressures constraining them. I say it would be difficult because it takes capital investment, industry knowledge, research, and trial and error all at enormous opportunity costs. There's no way stakeholders will take such risks without having a financial reward.

Let's look at socialized healthcare. It would stymie new innovations and leave market demand unrealized. What motivation is there for anyone to invent anything new? Even if some genius has an idea to develop something innovative, there's no financial reward so it may never see the light of day. Additionally, the government may not be interested due to its budget. Instead of being free to pursue profit in the healthcare market, individuals and enterprises with new products would have to apply to be a government contractor first. The government as a consequence becomes the sole customer instead of a wide and diverse marketplace.

Within a free market, even within a regulated industry like healthcare, businesses have the opportunity to satisfy demand and then either profit or fail. When people are unable to reap the financial rewards of hard work or for risk taking, then the needs of a market will go unmet.

Because the government would be the sole purchaser, it places the emphasis on satisfying the supply side. This would result in money being doled out for budget items and not necessarily for what the demand may actually be. The budget restraints of the government as sole buyer, instead of many willing buyers within a free market, will result in less invention and innovation. The country's healthcare would decline as a result.

The same would be true of every other industry. What incentive is there for anyone to meet the needs of a market without any reward? There may be exceptions, but for the most part, demand will go unfulfilled undermining the standard of living for all of society.

Stagnant Standard of Living

Market demand usually isn't shouting for something better to come along. It's quiet, utilizing what's already available. It's not until some supplier with a new product enters the marketplace that's better in some way, does demand shift. Many times, the consumer didn't even realize they would want the new product or service until it became known and available.

As a result of suppliers working hard to satisfy demand, the standard of living of society continually improves. Do you remember your grandmother's small appliances? They were made of steel and could survive a drop from a four-story building. When plastics became the material of choice, some critics would complain calling them junk because they weren't as well made. Possibly true, but they were more desirable because they were lighter, easier to handle and more affordable. Also, people didn't have the need to throw them out the window.

Does a steel iron being replaced by a plastic one improve society's standard of living? Why yes it does, in a small way perhaps. All incremental changes satisfying demand improve our standard of living. Products become less expensive freeing our disposable income for other goods or for organic wealth creation. Products also become better by providing more utility. New products and services are introduced besides, enhancing our lives, e.g., the automobile, Wi-Fi and smartphones.

Unmet market demand means supply isn't working to satisfy it because there's no financial reward. As a consequence, innovative or new products are never introduced to the market. And even more of a consequence, the standard of living for all of society stagnates.

A perfect example of socialism stagnating society's living standards is Cuba. Visiting Cuba is like taking a time machine back in history before Fidel Castro's led Cuban Revolution from 1953 to 1959.[3] In 2016, the New York Times called Cuba, "a country frozen in time."[4] And also, "The theme park that is Cuba is an insular museum, stuck between the Iron Curtain and the industrial capitalism of the 1950s."

Cuba stagnated for well over a half century because entrepreneurship and private property was removed from their economic system. There wasn't the ability for Cubans to pursue profit by meeting demand because they couldn't own productive property. Society owned the means of production, which is the same as saying society owned the income generated from that production.

Removing the profit motive in socialism takes away the need for enterprises to adapt, compete, innovate and invent for the purpose of earning the most income as possible. Without the need to pursue profit, there will obviously be less production, invention and innovation. The end result is a deficient market and a dormant standard of living for nearly everyone. The only exceptions are the ruling class, which gets their troughs filled up to the tippy top of everything other capitalist economies can produce.

Unequal Transactions

In free market capitalism, the economy is based on equal transactions. This means market participants rely upon the laws of supply and demand as the forces determining prices and wages. Consequently, the natural outcome for both sides of transactions is fair and equal.

These equal transactions, within a free market, are what motivate individuals and businesses to pursue profit. If an entity wants to earn income, they must provide something else of equal value which then fulfills demand. The wealth pie expands with organic wealth (unconsumed income) because it's the result of producing equal value for a marketplace.

Imagine this: a person cutting a sliver away from the wealth pie and using it to pay someone else for an equal value of labor. The production will be used by the employer to earn revenue which then replaces the amount previously sliced away. The wealth pie has exactly the same value as before. Now, though, the laborer can save some of their income and make the wealth pie bigger. The employer too can leverage the laborer's production to earn revenue and expand the wealth pie by saving any profit. Expanding wealth is only possible because of free market capitalism and its equal transactions.

Socialist systems are not made up of equal transactions. The laws of supply and demand are not the forces market participants rely upon. Instead, income is doled out to economic stakeholders in the form of a distribution unattached to a free market or providing equal value. Because income is distributed, any saved income just represents a wealth transfer since it was obtained without producing equal value to some other entity.

Product Prices

To understand why income is distributed, we first have to look at product prices within a democratic socialist economy. Determining pricing will be done by the stakeholders of an enterprise. If they were traditional business people, they would look at market demand to help in determining pricing. They would then produce goods at a cost, which would allow them to sell their product for a profit. Getting the cost right is essential for profitability.

Stakeholders, on the other hand, would not take market demand into account, at least not to the same extent. On account of the government guaranteeing a job for everyone, firms would be unable to have the ideal number of employees that's market based. In lieu of supply and demand forces, enterprises would be encouraged to have as many people as they could possibly squeeze in.

Additionally, firms would be required to provide a certain level of benefits, which government rulers would refer to as basic human rights. For these reasons, costs would only increase in firms run for the social good and not run to maximize earnings for its shareholders.

The effect, not surprisingly, will be bloated budgets. This will force firms to price products based on their costs rather than the force of consumer demand. If product prices are so high people cannot afford to purchase them, then the government will set price controls, which would necessitate the subsidizing of firms.

The outcome of prices based on bloated costs is unequal transactions. The production costs will be far greater than what the consumer would be willing to pay. Or, the consumer will pay what the actual production costs are for the product, but it's still not equal because there's no mechanism such as competition to bring prices down.

There'll be much less competition because that would eventually lead to winners and losers. Competition also results in creative destruction,[5] which is where one firm innovates, displacing older methods used by other firms.

Being a market loser or being replaced by a more innovative firm would lead to job losses. As expected, that's no way to manage an economy that works for everybody. So instead, only one firm will produce some product society needs. Possibly several firms doing the same thing could exist, but in cooperation with one another to prevent one from running the others out of business.

Salaries and Wages

Because product pricing in socialism isn't based on supply and demand from within a free market, it's also true salaries and wages would not be based on supply and demand either. In a free market, salaries and wages are part of the input costs for the final product and cannot be higher than the production value received in return. Otherwise, companies couldn't be profitable.

That's not true in democratic socialism. Revenue from product sales will be disconnected from wages and salaries. Wages will be determined by other factors such as fairness, the government's view of a living wage or some other notion of basic human rights. It will not be determined by the production value of each employee that's market based. How could it be based on production value when a firm isn't pursuing profit but just exists for the social good?

Because the production value of employees isn't the factor determining wages, a firm which could otherwise produce their products with ten workers, could actually have thirty, sixty or ninety workers. This would require a government subsidy, but it would be worth it to the Keynesian thinkers. According to their logic, investing in demand will lead to an equal value of supply, which will cause the need for the supply side to hire more workers.

Now, let's bring this home. In capitalism, income is received in exchange for an equal value of production. The company then uses that production to hopefully earn a profit. But in socialism, the income received is not the result of providing equal value to a firm. As mentioned, the worker's income is determined by other factors.

Whatever non-market reasoning is used to determine wages, it will be disconnected from a worker's production value. Income will merely be the result of distribution. Since each worker is an economic stakeholder and is an equal owner of society's means of production, they are entitled to their share of the available revenue.

In socialism, when a sliver is sliced away from the wealth pie to pay a worker, the labor doesn't replace what was removed. The reason is that the production provided by the worker isn't used by the firm to pursue profit or to even break even. If the firm did break even, without any government subsidy, the pie would be the same as before. But if the revenue of the firm isn't sufficient to effectively replace what it paid to its workers, due to a bloated budget, the wealth pie will just get smaller.

Finite Wealth Pie

Many proponents of socialism believe it's a fairer economic system, but in reality socialism attempts to rewrite human nature and it undoes natural market forces. Going against God's intent is what's actually unfair. They may desire an equitable outcome, but it comes at the expense of removing the motivation to bring something of value to the marketplace. As a result, everyone suffers the consequence of unmet market demand.

One of socialism's goals is to create a moral society where wealth is equally distributed. This may sound just to decent people, but in practice, the despair of the poor eventually spreads across all of society because the wealth pie becomes finite.

Equality is achieved for the masses, but to the detriment of a quality of life that's actually enjoyable. To say it another way, there are no rich or even a middle class because everyone ultimately becomes poor. That is the historical outcome of socialism around the world when revolutionaries took hold of power and made good on their promises.

Businesses create organic wealth in capitalism because of the incentive to make a profit. Not so in socialism. Enterprises will exist to produce income for consumption and nothing else. In democratic socialism, firms will never profit due to high labor costs, benefits and other compliance costs. By definition, there may not be any profit anyway because private ownership doesn't exist.

Any firm having revenue exceeding expenses will forward such amount to the government to cover shortfalls elsewhere. The bottom line is that the means of production will never expand the wealth pie in democratic socialism.

The other potential sources of wealth creation are individuals who receive an income. But in socialism, individuals will be limited in how much they can earn and accumulate. This will make organic wealth through saved income nearly impossible. Even if one can save some of their income, there'll be no investment opportunities to place that income. It will just steadily lose purchasing power due to inflation. As a consequence, earning an income will not expand the wealth pie because income will be used just for consumption and not for organic wealth creation.

To sum this up, the wealth pie will not grow anymore because a socialist society will own the means of production where profiting has been removed from the system. All production, therefore, will just be for consumption.

Additionally, earning too much by workers or small business owners will be prohibited and there won't be any investment opportunities anyway to create a gain. This all equates to a finite wealth pie where there's no additional wealth being created.

Eating the Pie

A finite wealth pie would be bad enough, but with socialism, no matter the variety, existing wealth doesn't just maintain itself. The remaining wealth begins to decline because the promised free stuff will require more than what's collected in tax revenue.

With the profit motive removed from the system, there will eventually be less production. In capitalism, people produce things for profiting's sake. In socialism, there's no incentive to produce anything that people may need or desire. Having less production will mean less income generation and with that, less revenue going to the government to pay for everything.

A democratic socialist government would promise to pay for everyone's basic human rights, e.g., education, health care, retirement, minimal housing, a basic income or a guaranteed job. Don't worry if your beloved "right" isn't listed, the government would no doubt cover a myriad of other necessities too.

The costs of such a society would be far greater than what the declining production would be. Additionally, with a guaranteed job or a basic income for everyone, many will live entirely off the system producing nothing of value in return. In order to pay for all the benefits and the newly found human rights the socialists will invent, they will have to look beyond the revenues collected from firms and individuals. Those sources will simply be insufficient to cover all the outlays.

The United States is currently very wealthy, but over time with democratic socialism, private net worth would either dissipate or be confiscated. The wealth which would be vanquished will be from transforming our economic system so that the means of production becomes publicly controlled rather than privately owned.

The value of publicly traded stocks, for instance, will go poof and become worthless. How the system would transition is debatable, but soon enough, any wealth from private ownership of the means of production will be gone. The exception may be a small business like a retail shop, but profits will be limited for its owners.

Of course, any wealth still in existence will eventually be confiscated with a wealth tax. The very wealthy will flee for another country like Sweden where their accumulated labor will be protected.

Taking wealth away from those who have too much is how the rulers will initially pay for all the goodies. It may be great at first, except for those who lose everything, but over time wealth will need to be confiscated from wherever it exists affecting nearly everyone. These assets will then be consumed.

Thus far, private wealth is no longer expanding and has mostly, if not entirely, been removed from the system. The state of the economy at that point will mainly consist of money that's circulating in the income/consumption pool. No buckets will be available though.

After those with wealth have been robbed thoroughly, any deficit in the budget will require the government to sell any assets that society owns, but which government controls. Selling off assets for shortfalls everywhere else will begin consuming the only remaining wealth, which consists of the country's natural resources.

Remember the blueberry pie mentioned in the beginning of the first chapter? I wrote that if wealth were a finite pie, then most people wouldn't be able to enjoy a full slice. The value of wealth would only consist of land and natural resources. These resources would need divvying up to pay for all the promises made. No doubt, they would be divided as fair as possible.

If democratic socialism is ever fully implemented, natural resources will be how wealth is calculated. Everything else we think of today that's included in an accounting of wealth would not exist. There will not be company stocks, investment accounts, private ownership of commercial real estate or any privately held non-personal land. Even your gold tooth better not be too big.

Most likely, the federal government, not stakeholders, will manage large industries such as fossil fuel production, earth mineral mining, metal ore excavation and big agriculture. To pay for all of society's benefits, it will require earnings from these industries to make up for the lack of revenues from individuals and enterprises.

Once the wealth tax has removed all excess wealth from individuals for consumption purposes, the government will only have global markets to raise additional revenue. It will have to rely on the large industries it manages to pay for all of the benefits that's been promised to every economic stakeholder as basic human rights.

If selling these products to a global market is somehow enough to cover all the expenses (and that's very doubtful), what will happen if commodity prices plummet or the population grows? There will be shortfalls again, but at that point, the only option will be to reduce benefits and product subsidies. In addition to lowering benefits, some socialist countries have chosen to invade and pillage other countries for their resources.

Democratic socialism leads directly to reduced production, which equals less revenue. A declining GDP will initially result in a stagnant standard of living. It wouldn't be long before our way of life begins to decline. Just like Cuba became frozen in time so too would the U.S. become stuck in the first half of the 21st century.

Eliminating organic wealth creation so the wealth pie can't expand is probably the most grievous mandate of socialism. Doing so causes the eating of the finite pie that remains just for survival. This is how the promised utopia fantasy comes to an end, and how the misery of the poor will eventually spread like a plague.

Afterword

Thank you for reading Organic Wealth. I hope you're inspired more than ever to begin creating organic wealth for yourself and your posterity. You should be well on your way to having principled reasons to choose free market capitalism over other ideas which advocate for more government control.

Knowing why you believe what you believe is especially necessary to oppose the movement of democratic socialism that's become very popular on the left. We're in an ideological battle with those who believe capitalism has failed us even though the world is much better off because of free markets than at any time in our history, notwithstanding the global pandemic.

With your firm footing and being intentional about creating organic wealth, the next greatest thing you can do with this book is to change other people's hearts and minds. By encouraging others with the principles and self-evident truths found in Organic Wealth, you will be spreading the virtues of free market capitalism and God's intent for us each to remain free. The more of us who have uncompromising free market principles, the stronger our Union will be.

Besides encouraging your family and friends to choose freedom and organic wealth creation, you may be inclined to go further. First, if you liked this book, please leave a positive review of where you purchased it. Your great review will help spread the word to others.

Second, subscribe to my newsletter at LibertyWord.com. You can read my responses to those who say a wealth tax is constitutional. Even though I'm not a lawyer, we can't let erroneous historical arguments go unanswered.

Third, receive more value by taking the Organic Wealth Bootcamp course. It's a journey that most can do leading to financial independence. See it at OrganicWealth.net.

Another positive action is to support a Convention of States so that we can place a strong check on the federal government. Sign the petition at conventionofstates.com.

Well, we've finally reached the end of this book. Even so it's just the beginning for organic wealth readers. You are now equipped to create your own slice of pie.

Remember, only within free market capitalism are people self-empowered to improve their lives. This is the American Dream. Since we still have the liberty to create organic wealth, all that's required is earning an income by fulfilling demand. So if you see it out there, go and get it!

Endnotes

Introduction

[1] "Global Wealth Report." Credit Suisse, www.credit-suisse.com/about-us/en/reports-research/global-wealth-report.html

1: Wealth is Created

[1] "Living Paycheck to Paycheck..., According to New CareerBuilder Survey." August 24, 2017. http://press.careerbuilder.com/2017-08-24-Living-Paycheck-to-Paycheck-is-a-Way-of-Life-for-Majority-of-U-S-Workers-According-to-New-CareerBuilder-Survey

[2] S&P Dow Jones Indices LLC, S&P/Case-Shiller U.S. National Home Price Index [CSUSHPISA], retrieved from FRED, Federal Reserve Bank of St. Louis, Nov. 30, 2021. https://fred.stlouisfed.org/series/CSUSHPISA

[3] "Kitty Sales." Dec. 14, 2021. https://kittysales.co

2: Equal Transactions

[1] "Look Back at Oprah's Free-Car Giveaway." Oprah.com, http://www.oprah.com/oprahshow/oprahs-entire-audience-are-surprised-with-new-cars-video

[2] Muresianu, Alex. "Yes, the U.S. Tax Code Is Progressive." Tax Foundation, 17 Sept. 2021, Date accessed Dec. 14, 2021
https://taxfoundation.org/us-tax-system-progressive

[3] Feuerherd, Ben. "Ocasio-Cortez: System That Allows Billionaires Is 'Immoral'." New York Post, 22 Jan. 2019, https://nypost.com/2019/01/22/ocasio-cortez-system-that-allows-billionaires-is-immoral

[4] Sunderland, Ruth, and Matt Oliver. "Nobody Deserves to Be This Rich - Bill Gates." IOL News, 14 Feb. 2019, https://www.iol.co.za/news/world/nobody-deserves-to-be-this-rich-bill-gates-19277011

[5] Spectrem Group's 2020 Report Reveals US Household... https://spectrem.com/Content_Press/spectrem-press-release-march-15-2021.aspx

3: Unlimited Wealth

[1] Gold Reserve Act of 1934. Federal Reserve History. www.federalreservehistory.org/essays/gold-reserve-act.

[2] Does the Federal Reserve Print Money?, Federal Reserve Bank of St. Louis, www.stlouisfed.org/open-

vault/2017/november/does-federal-reserve-print-money

[3] Chappelow, Jim. "M2 Definition." Investopedia, https://www.investopedia.com/terms/m/m2.asp

[4] "M2 Money Stock." FRED, Nov. 23, 2021, https://fred.stlouisfed.org/series/M2SL

[5] Velocity of M2 Money Stock." FRED, 24 Nov. 2021, https://fred.stlouisfed.org/series/M2V

[6] "Amazon Trillion: Company Follows..." CNNMoney, https://money.cnn.com/2018/09/04/technology/amazon-1-trillion/index.html

[7] Caplinger, Dan. "Will 2019 Be Amazon's Dividend Debut?" The Motley Fool, 15 Jan. 2019, https://www.fool.com/investing/2019/01/14/will-2019-be-amazons-dividend-debut.aspx

[8] "HOUSEHOLD DEBT AND CREDIT REPORT (Q3 2021)." FEDERAL RESERVE BANK of NEW YORK, https://www.newyorkfed.org/microeconomics/hhdc.html

4: Effective Supply

[1] Pomerleau, Kyle. "The Treatment of Foreign Profits... The Tax Foundation, www.taxfoundation.org/treatment-foreign-profits-tax-cuts-jobs-act

[2] Laffer, Arthur. "The Laffer Curve: Past, Present, and Future." The Heritage Foundation,

https://www.heritage.org/taxes/report/the-laffer-curve-past-present-and-future

[3] Kessler, Glenn. "Analysis | Rand Paul's Claim That Reagan's Tax Cuts Produced 'More Revenue' and 'Tens of Millions of Jobs'." Washington Post, 12 Nov. 2021, https://www.washingtonpost.com/news/fact-checker/wp/2015/04/10/rand-pauls-claim-that-reagans-tax-cuts-produced-more-revenue-and-tens-of-millions-of-jobs

[4] "Republican Party Founded." History.com, A&E Television Networks, 9 Feb. 2010, https://www.history.com/this-day-in-history/republican-party-founded

[5] "Founders Online: To Thomas Jefferson from Jean Baptiste Say, 2 Nov 1803." Nat Archives & Rec. Admin. https://founders.archives.gov/documents/Jefferson/01-41-02-0486

[6] Kanopiadmin. "A Treatise on Political Economy: Jean-Baptiste Say." Mises Institute, 18 Aug. 2014, https://mises.org/library/treatise-political-economy

[7] "Founders Online: Jean Baptiste Say to Thomas Jefferson, 15 June 1814." Nat Archive & Records Admin. https://founders.archives.gov/documents/Jefferson/03-07-02-0308

[8] "Founders Online: Thomas Jefferson to Jean Baptiste Say, 2 March 1815." Nat. Archive and Records Admin.,

https://founders.archives.gov/documents/Jefferson/03-08-02-0242

9 Sowell, Thomas. On Classical Economics. Yale University Pr., 2009, p. 73.

10 Kanopiadmin. "A Treatise on Political Economy: Jean-Baptiste Say." Mises Institute, 18 Aug. 2014, p. 287, https://mises.org/library/treatise-political-economy

11 "Consumer Price Index, 1913-." Fed Reserve of Min, https://www.minneapolisfed.org/about-us/monetary-policy/inflation-calculator/consumer-price-index-1913-

12 Budget FY 2020 - Table 1.1 -Summary of Receipts, Outlays, and Surpluses or Deficits: 1789–2024, https://www.govinfo.gov/app/details/BUDGET-2020-TAB/BUDGET-2020-TAB-2-1/context

13 "Discount Rates, Federal Reserve Bank of New York for United States." FRED, 20 Aug. 2012, https://fred.stlouisfed.org/series/M13009USM156NNBR

14 "A History of the Federal Reserve, Volume 1: 1913-1951." Federal Reserve Bank of Minneapolis, https://www.minneapolisfed.org/article/2003/a-history-of-the-federal-reserve-volume-1-19131951

15 "Consumer Price Index, 1913-." Consumer Price Index, 1913- | Federal Reserve Bank of Minneapolis, https://www.minneapolisfed.org/about-us/monetary-policy/inflation-calculator/consumer-price-index-1913-

[16] "The Measurement and Behavior of Unemployment." NBER, 1 Jan. 1957, Annual Estimates of Unemployment in the United States, 1900-1954: Stanley Lebergott (p. 211 - 242), https://www.nber.org/books/univ57-1

[17] "Entrepreneurship." The Economist, https://www.economist.com/news/2009/04/27/entrepreneurship

[18] "The General Theory Of Employment, Interest And Money : John Maynard Keynes." 1 Jan. 1970, p. 18, https://archive.org/details/TheGeneralTheoryOfEmploymentInterestAndMoney_201707

[19] Ibid., p. 22.

[20] Ibid., p. 26.

[21] Kanopiadmin. "A Treatise on Political Economy: Jean-Baptiste Say." Mises Institute, 18 Aug. 2014, p. 135, https://mises.org/library/treatise-political-economy

[22] Ibid., p. 133, footnote.

[23] Ibid., p. 139.

[24] The Great Depression. Nat Archives & Records Admin., https://hoover.archives.gov/exhibits/great-depression

[25] "Discount Rates, Federal Reserve Bank of New York for United States." FRED, 20 Aug. 2012, https://fred.stlouisfed.org/series/M13009USM156NNBR

[26] Budget FY 2020 - Table 1.1 - Summary of Receipts, Outlays, and Surpluses or Deficits (–): 1789–2024, https://www.govinfo.gov/app/details/BUDGET-2020-TAB/BUDGET-2020-TAB-2-1/context

[27] Klein, Christopher. "Before FDR, Herbert Hoover Tried His Own 'New Deal'." History.com, 28 Feb. 2019, https://www.history.com/news/great-depression-herbert-hoover-new-deal

[28] "Books / Digital Text." Mises Institute, https://mises.org/library/progressive-era-0/html/c/631

[29] "Smoot-Hawley Tariff Act." Encyclopedia Britannica, Dec. 2021, https://www.britannica.com/topic/Smoot-Hawley-Tariff-Act

[30] Horwitz, Steven, et al. "Hoover's Economic Policies." https://www.econlib.org/library/Enc/HooversEconomicPolicies.html

[31] "New Deal Policies and the Persistence of the Great Depression: A General Equilibrium Analysis." Federal Reserve Bank of Minneapolis, https://www.minneapolisfed.org/research/working-papers/new-deal-policies-and-the-persistence-of-the-great-depression-a-general-equilibrium-analysis

[32] GDP and Other Major NIPA Series, 1929–2011: II, Bureau of Economic Analysis, Percentages were calculated using the data from Table 1,

https://apps.bea.gov/scb/pdf/2011/08%20August/0811_gdp_nipas.pdf

[33] Higgs, Robert. “Regime Uncertainty: Why the Great Depression Lasted So Long and Why Prosperity Resumed after the War.” The Independent Review, vol. 1, no. 4, 1997, pp. 561–590. JSTOR, www.jstor.org/stable/24560785

[34] What Caused the Great Depression? Foundation for Economic Education, 2 Feb. 2018, https://fee.org/articles/what-caused-the-great-depression

[35] Chappelow, Jim. “How the Circular Flow Of Income Model Works.” Investopedia, 9 Feb. 2021, https://www.investopedia.com/terms/circular-flow-of-income.asp

[36] Boyer, Dave. “'Thanks, Obama!' Former President Credits Himself for Strong Economy.” The Washington Times, 6 Dec. 2017, https://www.washingtontimes.com/news/2017/dec/6/thanks-obama-former-president-credits-himself-stro

[37] “Paul Krugman: The Economic Fallout.” The New York Times, 9 Nov. 2016, https://www.nytimes.com/interactive/projects/cp/opinion/election-night-2016/paul-krugman-the-economic-fallout

[38] “Bureau of Labor Statistics Data,” https://data.bls.gov/timeseries/LNS14000000/

[39] U.S. Bureau of Labor Statistics, https://www.bls.gov/charts/employment-situation/civilian-labor-force-participation-rate.htm

[40] Meredith, Sam. "'Major Milestone': US Could Become a Sustained Net Oil Exporter as Soon as next Year, IEA Says." CNBC, 12 Dec. 2019, https://www.cnbc.com/2019/12/12/oil-us-could-become-a-sustained-net-exporter-in-late-2020-iea-says.html

"U.S. Energy Information Administration - EIA - Independent Statistics and Analysis." U.S. Petroleum Exports Exceed Imports in September, https://eia.gov/todayinenergy/detail.php?id=42176

[41] Gross Output, https://grossoutput.com/gross-output

5: Private Property

[1] Lea, Brittany De. "Sanders Calls for 'National Wealth Registry' to Support Extreme Tax on Rich." Fox Business, 29 Sept. 2019, https://www.foxbusiness.com/money/sanders-national-wealth-registry-tax-rich

[2] Heath, F. Eugene. "Invisible Hand." Encyclopedia Britannica, 12 Dec. 2017, https://www.britannica.com/topic/invisible-hand

[3] "Obama to Business Owners: 'You Didn't Build That'." Fox News, 27 Jan. 2015,

https://www.foxnews.com/politics/obama-to-business-owners-you-didnt-build-that

6: Power Restrained

[1] Avalon Project - Articles of Confederation: March 1, 1781, https://avalon.law.yale.edu/18th_century/artconf.asp

[2] James Madison's Notes of the constitutional Convention (May 29, 1787), https://www.consource.org/document/james-madisons-notes-of-the-constitutional-convention-1787-5-29/#28

[3] History.com. “Shays' Rebellion.” 12 Nov. 2009, https://history.com/topics/early-us/shays-rebellion

[4] Berkeley Electronic Press. "What the Constitution Means by "Duties, Imposts, and Excises"-and "Taxes" (Direct or Otherwise)" by Robert G. Natelson, https://works.bepress.com/robert_natelson/39

[5] Hamilton, Alexander. The Federalist No. 21 (December 12, 1787), https://www.consource.org/document/the-federalist-no-21-1787-12-12/#12

[6] The Federalist No. 40 (January 18, 1788), https://www.consource.org/document/the-federalist-no-40-1788-1-18/#14

[7] Ely, Richard T. Taxation in American States and Cities: Assisted by John h. Finley. 1888, p. 109.

[8] History.com. "Stamp Act." 9 Nov. 2009, https://www.history.com/topics/american-revolution/stamp-act

[9] "Founding.com." A Project of the Claremont Institute, http://founding.com/founders-library/government-documents/british-government-documents-2/examination-of-dr-benjamin-franklin-in-the-house-of-commons

[10] The Debates in the Several State Conventions of the Adoption of the Federal Constitution, Vol. 2 (Mass., Conn., NH, NY, Penn, Maryland) – Online Library of Liberty, https://oll.libertyfund.org/titles/1906#Elliot_1314-02_922

[11] The Debates in the Several State Conventions of the Adoption of the Federal Constitution, Vol. 3 (Virginia) - Online Library of Liberty, https://oll.libertyfund.org/titles/1907#Elliot_1314-03_408

[12] "Capitation: Search Online Etymology Dictionary." https://www.etymonline.com/search?q=capitation

[13] "Poll: Search Online Etymology Dictionary." https://www.etymonline.com/search?q=poll

[14] An Inquiry Into the Nature and Causes of the Wealth of Nations (Cannan Ed.), Vol. 2 - Online Lib. of Liberty, https://oll.libertyfund.org/titles/119#Smith_0206-02_864

[15] https://www.britannica.com/topic/capitation

[16] An Inquiry Into the Nature and Causes of the Wealth of Nations (Cannan Ed.), Vol. 2 - Online Lib. of Liberty, https://oll.libertyfund.org/titles/119#Smith_0206-02_868

[17] The Dissent of the Minority of the Pennsylvania Convention, Pennsylvania Packet (December 18, 1787), https://www.consource.org/document/the-dissent-of-the-minority-of-the-pennsylvania-convention-pennsylvania-packet-1787-12-18

[18] The Debates in the Several State Conventions of the Adoption of the Fed. Const., Vol. 1 - Online Lib. of Liberty, https://oll.libertyfund.org/titles/1905#Elliot_1314-01_3481

[19] James Madison's Notes of the constitutional Convention (May 29, 1787), https://www.consource.org/document/james-madisons-notes-of-the-constitutional-convention-1787-5-29/#29

[20] The Debates on the Adoption of the Federal Constitution in the Convention Held at Philadelphia in 1787, Vol. 5 (Debates in Congress, Madison's Notes, Misc. Letters), https://oll.libertyfund.org/titles/1909#Elliot_1314-05_2718

[21] https://oll.libertyfund.org/titles/1909#Elliot_1314-05_2748

[22] https://oll.libertyfund.org/titles/1909#Elliot_1314-05_2734

[23] James Madison's Notes of the constitutional Convention (September 14, 1787), https://www.consource.org/document/james-madisons-notes-of-the-constitutional-convention-1787-9-14/#54

[24] Delegates to the Constitutional Conv.: George Read, https://teachingamericanhistory.org/static/convention/delegates/read.html

7: Taking by Tax

[1] "... An Act Laying Duties upon Carriages for the Conveyance of Persons. [Philadelphia: Printed by Childs and Swaine, 1794.]." The Library of Congress, https://www.loc.gov/item/rbpe.2210010e

[2] February Term, 1796. Hylton, Plaintiff in Error, v. the United States. On the 4th of February, a Commission, Bearing Date the 27th. Legal Information Institute, https://law.cornell.edu/supremecourt/text/3/171

[3] "Pacific Ins. v. Soule, 74 U.S. 433 (1868)." Justia Law, https://supreme.justia.com/cases/federal/us/74/433

[4] "Veazie Bank v. Fenno, 75 U.S. 533 (1869)." Justia Law, https://supreme.justia.com/cases/federal/us/75/533

[5] "Scholey v. Rew, 90 U.S. 331 (1874)." Justia Law, https://supreme.justia.com/cases/federal/us/90/331

[6] "Springer v. U.S., 102 U.S. 586 (1880)." Justia Law, https://supreme.justia.com/cases/federal/us/102/586

[7] "Excise (n.)." Index, https://www.etymonline.com/word/excise

[8] "Pollock v. Farmers' Loan & Trust Company, Page 158 U.S. 601 (1895)." Justia Law, https://supreme.justia.com/cases/federal/us/158/601

[9] Ibid., Page 158 U. S. 637. https://supreme.justia.com/cases/federal/us/158/601

[10] "Nicol v. Ames, 173 U.S. 509 (1899)." Justia Law, https://supreme.justia.com/cases/federal/us/173/509

[11] "Thomas v. United States, 192 U.S. 363 (1904)." Justia Law, https://supreme.justia.com/cases/federal/us/192/363

[12] "Knowlton v. Moore, 178 U.S. 41 (1900)." Justia Law, https://supreme.justia.com/cases/federal/us/178/41

"New York Trust Co. v. Eisner, 256 U.S. 345 (1921)." Justia Law, https://supreme.justia.com/cases/federal/us/256/345

[13] "Flint v. Stone Tracy Co., 220 U.S. 107 (1911)." Justia, https://supreme.justia.com/cases/federal/us/220/107

[14] "Bromley v. McCaughn, 280 U.S. 124 (1929)." Justia, https://supreme.justia.com/cases/federal/us/280/124

[15] "Five Items Congress Deleted from Madison's Original Bill of Rights." National Constitution Center – Constitutioncenter.org, https://constitutioncenter.org/blog/five-items-congress-deleted-from-madisons-original-bill-of-rights

[16] James Madison's Proposed Amendments to the Constitution, June 8, 1789, National Archives and Records Administration, www.archives.gov/files/legislative/resources/education/bill-of-rights/images/handout-2.pdf

8: Democratic Socialism

[1] "What Is Democratic Socialism?" Democratic Socialists of America (DSA), https://www.dsausa.org/about-us/what-is-democratic-socialism

[2] What Is a Worker Cooperative? | Democracy at Work Institute, https://institute.coop/what-worker-cooperative

[3] "What Striking Autoworkers Want from General Motors." CBS News, CBS Interactive, https://www.cbsnews.com/news/why-are-united-auto-workers-on-strike-against-gm

[4] Biden unveils economic plan, calls for end to shareholder capitalism. (n.d.). May 06, 2021, https://www.yahoo.com/lifestyle/biden-unveils-economic-plan-calls-153218779.html

[5] AB-5 Worker Status: Employees & Contractors, Sec. 2, https://leginfo.legislature.ca.gov/faces/billNavClient.xhtml?bill_id=201920200AB5

[6] Barrabi, Thomas. "NBA Moving Away from 'Owner' in Favor of 'Governor,'..." Fox Business, 24 June 2019, https://www.foxbusiness.com/features/nba-adam-silver-owner-title

[7] Stevens, John Paul. Six Amendments: How and Why We Should Change the Constitution. Little, Brown and Company, 2014.

[8] "USAspending.gov." USAspending.gov, https://usaspending.gov/#/explorer/budget_function

[9] "How Sweden Created a Model Economy." 2 Nov. 2018 https://web.archive.org/web/20181102163007/https://sweden.se/business/how-sweden-created-a-model-economy/

[10] "2021 Index of Economic Freedom," https://www.heritage.org/index

[11] Asen, Elke. "Top Individual Income Tax Rates in Europe." Tax Foundation, 2 Oct. 2019, https://taxfoundation.org/top-individual-income-tax-rates-europe-2019

[12] Asen, Elke. "VAT Rates in Europe: Value-Added Tax: European Rankings." Tax Foundation, 2 Oct. 2019, https://taxfoundation.org/vat-rates-europe-2019

[13] List of Countries by Corporate Tax Rate, https://tradingeconomics.com/country-list/corporate-tax-rate

9: Beyond Nordic

[1] Wiles, David. "Swedes and Taxes." https://web.archive.org/web/20210813032522/https://sweden.se/society/why-swedes-are-okay-with-paying-taxes/

[2] Michaels, Matthew. "How Much the Average Person in 40 Different Countries Takes Home after Taxes." Business Insider, Business Insider, 16 May 2018, https://www.businessinsider.com/tax-rates-take-home-salaries-40-countries-2018-5. #39

[3] Accountable Capitalism Act | U.S. Senator Elizabeth Warren of Massachusetts, 15 Aug. 2018, https://www.warren.senate.gov/newsroom/press-releases/warren-introduces-accountable-capitalism-act

[4] "Benefit Corporation." State by State Status of Legislation | Benefit Corporation, https://benefitcorp.net/policymakers/state-by-state-status

[5] "Fortune 500." Fortune, 12 May 2021, https://fortune.com/fortune500/2020/search

[6] Warren Joins Baldwin, Colleagues in Effort to Give Workers a Greater Voice at Public Companies: U.S. Sen. Elizabeth Warren of Massachusetts. 16 Oct. 2018,

https://www.warren.senate.gov/oversight/letters/warren-joins-baldwin-colleagues-in-effort-to-give-workers-a-greater-voice-at-public-companies

[7] Ocasio-Cortez, Alexandria. "Text - H.Res.109 - 116th Congress (2019-2020): Recognizing the Duty of the Federal Government to Create a Green New Deal." Congress.gov, 12 Feb. 2019, https://www.congress.gov/bill/116th-congress/house-resolution/109

[8] Markey, and Edward J. "S.Res.59 - 116th Congress (2019-2020): A Resolution Recognizing the Duty of the Federal Government..." Congress.gov, 7 Feb. 2019, https://www.congress.gov/bill/116th-congress/senate-resolution/59

[9] McConnell, Mitch. "S.J.Res.8 - 116th Congress (2019-2020): A Joint Resolution Recognizing the Duty of the Federal Government to Create a Green New Deal." Congress.gov, 26 Mar. 2019, https://www.congress.gov/bill/116th-congress/senate-joint-resolution/8

[10] "Jobs for All." Bernie Sanders - Official Website, https://berniesanders.com/issues/jobs-for-all

[11] Booker, and Cory A. "S.2746 - 115th Congress (2017-2018): Federal Jobs Guarantee Development Act of 2018." Congress.gov, 25 Apr. 2018, https://www.congress.gov/bill/115th-congress/senate-bill/2746

[12] "What Is Universal Basic Income? - Yang2020 - Andrew Yang for President." Yang2020, https://yang2020.com/what-is-freedom-dividend-faq

[13] "Finland's Basic Income Trial Boosted Well-Being, but Not Employment." HelsinkiTimes, 8 Feb. 2019, https://www.helsinkitimes.fi/finland/finland-news/domestic/16182-finland-s-basic-income-trial-boosted-well-being-but-not-employment.html

[14] "The De Blasio Fair Share Tax Plan." De Blasio, https://billdeblasio.com/fair-share-tax-plan

[15] "Tax on Extreme Wealth." Bernie Sanders - Official Campaign Website, https://berniesanders.com/issues/tax-extreme-wealth

[16] Sanders, Bernie. "There Should Be No Billionaires. We Are Going to Tax Their Extreme Wealth and Invest in Working People. Twitter, 24 Sept. 2019, https://twitter.com/BernieSanders/status/1176485327336329216

[17] "Ultra-Millionaire Tax." Elizabeth Warren, https://elizabethwarren.com/ultra-millionaire-tax

[18] "Ending the Stranglehold of Health Care Costs on American Families." Elizabeth Warren, https://elizabethwarren.com/plans/paying-for-m4a

[19] "Warren, Jayapal, Boyle Introduce Ultra-Millionaire Tax on Fortunes Over $50 Million" 1 Mar. 2021,

https://www.warren.senate.gov/newsroom/press-releases/warren-jayapal-boyle-introduce-ultra-millionaire-tax-on-fortunes-over-50-million

20 Quinnipiac University. "National (US)." QU Poll, https://poll.qu.edu/national

21 Madani, Doha. "'I'd Take the Wall down,' Says Beto O'Rourke of Current Border Barriers." NBCNews.com, NBCUniversal News Group, 15 Feb. 2019, https://www.nbcnews.com/news/us-news/i-d-take-wall-down-says-beto-o-rourke-current-n971896

22 Kurtzleben, Danielle, et al. "Immigration: Where 2020 Democratic Candidates Stand On Border Crossings And More." NPR, 12 Sept. 2019, https://www.npr.org/2019/09/12/759442642/immigration-where-2020-democratic-candidates-stand-on-border-crossings-and-more

23 Hains, Tim. "Sen. Kamala Harris: Time To 'Reexamine ICE And Its Role.'" RealClearPolitics, https://realclearpolitics.com/video/2018/06/25/sen_kamala_harris_time_to_reexamine_ice_and_its_role.html

24 "Sweden Slashes Refugee Forecast Figures for 2016." The Local, 27 Apr. 2016, https://www.thelocal.se/20160427/swedens-migration-agency-slashes-refugee-forecast

25 Schwartz, Ian. "All Democrats At Main Debate Agree Illegal Immigrants Should Get Health Care Coverage."

https://realclearpolitics.com/video/2019/06/27/all_dem_candidates_raise_hand_when_asked_if_illegal_immigrants_should_get_health_care_coverage_at_debate.html

26 Chasmar, Jessica. “Bernie Sanders Defines 'Democratic Socialism,' Says Living Wage and Free College Are 'Human Rights'.” AP NEWS, Associated Press, 26 Feb. 2019, https://apnews.com/f1b18e4a6a652a4f651a9915bf8d237f

10: Zero Sum Wealth

1 Ramsey Solutions. “Tired of Keeping Up with the Joneses?” Daveramsey.com, 20 June 2019, https://www.daveramsey.com/blog/tired-of-keeping-up-with-the-joneses

2 “Financial Peace University.” FPU: The Proven Personal Finance Plan | DaveRamsey.com, https://www.daveramsey.com/fpu

3 “Fidel Castro.” History.com, 9 Nov. 2009, https://www.history.com/topics/cold-war/fidel-castro

4 Álvarez, Carlos Manuel. “Cuba, a Country Frozen in Time.” The New York Times, 15 July 2016, https://www.nytimes.com/2016/07/16/opinion/cuba-a-country-frozen-in-time.html

5 1883-1950. “Joseph Alois Schumpeter.” Econlib, https://econlib.org/library/Enc/bios/Schumpeter.html

eBook

Organic Wealth is available digitally.

Download a perfectly formatted copy for your E-Reader today!

Please visit the online store where you purchased this book for your copy or by going to OrganicWealth.net.

Made in the USA
Monee, IL
04 November 2026

67387536R00174